Foreword By
THE Hovering Game
How to Change Helicopter Parenting Behaviour in Youth Sports
SHANE DONEN

The Hovering Game

How to Change Helicopter Parenting Behaviour in Youth Sports

Shane Donen

Published by CreateSpace.com

This edition published in Canada by Pursuit MS
www.helicopterparenting.net.

Library and Archives Canada Cataloguing in Publication

Donen, Shane, author
The hovering game: how to change helicopter parenting behaviour in youth sports / Shane Donen.

Issued in print and electronic formats.
ISBN 978-0-9939231-3-5 (paperback).
ISBN 978-0-9939231-4-2 (kindle).
ISBN 978-0-9939231-5-9 (epub).

1. Sports for children. 2. Parenting. I. Title.

GV709.2.D65 2016 796.083 C2016-904339-8
C2016-904340-1

Editing: Note Editorial and Publishing Services
noteeditorialandpublishing.ca

Typography: Susan Sullivan, FMS Creative
fmscreative.com

Illustrations: Mallory Donen
artbymallorydonen.ca

For more information, visit helicopterparenting.net

For my mother

Priscilla,

who inspired me to dream.

Remember this. Hold on to this.
This is the only perfection there is, the perfection of
helping others. This is the only thing we can do
that has any lasting meaning. This is why we're here.

—Andre Agassi

TABLE OF CONTENTS

CHAPTER 5—*What Do the Kids Think?*

CHAPTER 6—*The Religion of Hockey*

CHAPTER 7—*Pro-Parents: Legacy Pros*

CHAPTER 8—*The Pursuit of Varsity College Sports*

CHAPTER 9—*Ode to the Parent Coach*

FOREWORD

I FIRST MET SHANE AT SIMON FRASER UNIVERSITY BACK IN THE EARLY 1980S WHEN I was helping out with the women's varsity volleyball team. He and a group of young men called the Fifty-Niners (guys who were 5'9" and under) would come out once a week to play some exhibition games against our team. Shane and many of his teammates were high flyers with big vertical jumps; they gave our girls lots of trouble, but helped the team with their competitive development.

Through the years I have witnessed Shane's passion for people through his work, coaching and family life. He and his wife Maryanne have raised three respectful and delightful children. When Shane came to me with the idea of writing a book about helicopter parenting, he had in fact already written the first draft. Just like him. When he gets a hold of a concept, he knows how to make it happen.

The Hovering Game is a must read for every parent who has or is thinking about having their child involved in organized sport. Shane has applied his unique insights as a coach, parent and administrator to tackle the helicopter parenting issue so common in youth sport today. His goal is simple: to affect change from the bottom up, one parent at a time. Shane's passion for helping people is infectious and motivating. He is one of those key people in the community who is an integral part of the village that raises the child.

This book will help parents to be aware of the helicopter traps by offering practical, helpful tips on how to stay away from them, and to get themselves or others out of them if they are caught. This book is grounded in the heart, created with love and with the hope that it will make a difference by helping parents preserve their relationships with their kids while supporting their love of play.

Our children and grandchildren deserve to be supported and nurtured through sport to be healthy, happy and competent citizens, loving the game and feeling good about themselves along the way. This book can and will help change helicopter parenting behaviour and make a difference for current and future generations of parents!

Rick Hansen, C.C., O.B.C.

PREFACE

> "Parenting is the easiest thing in the world to have an opinion about, but the hardest thing in the world to do."
>
> —*Matt Walsh, American Comedian*

YOU'VE LIKELY HEARD THE STATEMENT "PARENTS TODAY ARE LIVING VICARIOUSLY through their children." When parents behave this way, they are labelled as "helicopter parents" because they hover over their kids' lives and activities. But do helicopter parents really exist? Of course they do! Everyone knows a heli-parent. The ultimate question is, are you a helicopter parent or are you living in denial? A more prevalent problem is many parents don't even realize that they are playing the Hovering Game with their own children, and some who have accepted at some level that they are helicopter parents, continue with this behaviour anyway, because they think it's okay.

Is the helicopter parenting phenomenon in our society getting worse? I believe so. Maybe not epidemic, but it is certainly growing at a rate that seems to gain momentum with every new generation of parents. And while the problem exists in parenting children during their education, leisure and social activities, never has it been more pronounced than in organized youth sport. Whether it is with boys or girls, team or individual sport, your nation's pastime or the latest in-vogue sport activity, helicoptering exists across the board. And those doing it think it helps, but it doesn't. Kids simply don't respond well to supplementary coaching by their parents. This behaviour negatively impacts the future relationship between you and your child. And you don't want this to happen!

The Hovering Game will help the heli-parents who are caught in the cyclone spinning over their kids. This book has been written to help identify the parent helicopter pilot in you and bring you safely down to earth. It is for the new parent eyeing their children's future sport activities, presenting them with a balanced approach to parenting their kids in organized sport. It is for the parent who currently has children in sports and who needs to gauge how badly they hover. It is for the parent who has recognized their "Aha" moment, when they crossed into hover territory, and wants to stay out of trouble. It is for the parent who may be burning their bridge of love and trust with their child, right before they leave the nest. It is for the parent who wants to help their spouse or friend who is living their sports dream through their children. *The Hovering Game* is for those who want their kids to continue loving them as much as they love their kids.

As a long-time coach and executive director in youth sport, a consultant for athletes moving on to play post-secondary sports and a veteran parent of three (now adult) children, I have spent much of my life mentoring and helping families find balance between loving sport, understanding the benefits of being competitive and growing love within their family unit. My passion to help and effect change is my motivation to write this book.

Using research and the findings from diverse focus groups, *The Hovering Game* will help the reader understand how to identify the traits of hovering, how some parents reach the point of helicoptering, the dos and don'ts to avoid helicoptering and most importantly, how to implement change.

If there was ever a reason to doubt whether I needed to write, it was confirmed for me during the parent focus group sessions conducted for my research. In almost every session, when participants were asked if they were helicopter parents, they initially answered no. But as the discussion continued, each would share an "Aha" moment that revealed some level of excessive hovering behaviour. Like the mother who nudged her husband at one of the sessions and challenged his behaviour—passing notes to their son during games through the team manager with instructions on what to do. You should have seen the look on his face when his wife exposed him on that reveal! Eventually, all the parents discovered some heli-parenting behaviours of their own. At first they felt a bit ashamed, yet at the same time relieved and invigorated. Hovering is really just parenting that has gone a bit too far. At the end of each session, participants were told what the book topic was. The most overwhelming response by the majority of participants is best articulated as, "A book on helicopter parenting in youth sports? Now that's a book we need! Our community needs a wake-up call!" These focus group sessions validated my inspiration.

Our parents' generation rarely exercised the level of open communication that is encouraged and practiced in today's society. As a parent, you are actively involved and present in all aspects of raising your child, however you don't want to lose your emotional attachment with them, do you? If you want to improve your future relationship with your child, and youth sport is part of your family life, I would like to help you!

Your child's time in organized youth sport will only last ten years or so, and trust me, the time flies by. Before you know it, they have gone to college or entered the workforce. Young adults want to leave home and prove their ability to be independent. If you want to maintain and grow your relationship with your son or daughter, and you aren't sure if you are a helicopter parent, read the book while you still have your kids living with you!

I wrote this book for those who like an easy read. I include true stories told with humour and love from the past and present and from a multitude of sport disciplines, and I am determined to help you help someone else, or help yourself. Each chapter will tell relevant stories, identify the problems and offer advice and solutions. You may disagree with some of what has been written, but at the very least, *The Hovering Game* will spark dialogue, thought and reflection. Have I piqued your curiosity yet? If so, read on!

INTRODUCTION

ALL PARENTS HOVER. IT'S IN OUR BLOOD, PART OF OUR GENETICS. IT STARTS THE moment your child is born. You did it the day you brought your child home from the hospital, plunked the car seat carrier in the middle of the living room and stood over top of him or her with joy, happiness and fear. You hovered when you put your child to bed and twenty minutes later, snuck back into the bedroom and put your finger up to their nose to make sure they were still breathing. You hovered when they crawled up the stairs for the first time, and cringed when they turned back to look at you—hoping they wouldn't fall! You hovered when you dropped them off at kindergarten and stayed for minutes after, looking through the classroom door window just to see if they were getting along with the other tots.

But when you take things too far, in any of your parenting skills, that is helicopter parenting. But who determines "too far?" How do you know when you have crossed the line? In some ways, our communities, societies and governments set the standards, but raising a child is still ultimately the parents' responsibility. Often it is just common sense, but it can be blurred by parental instincts, love, passion and dreams of a better life for your children.

When you enter your kids into a sports program for the first time, the challenge can be even more daunting. We are afraid—they could get hurt, they won't get along with others, they won't like the instructor, and they won't be good enough. The fear of harm, not fitting in, authority and failure. Should I stay at practice to make sure everything is all right? Should I sit in the stands to cheer them on at a game? Should I immediately run to them if they skin their knee? What should I do? That is the beginning of the Hovering Game.

The Hovering Game is a compilation of my stories and the stories of others turned into a self-help guide for youth sport parents. Together we'll learn from our past, and why youth sport is a necessary part of your kid's life. We'll define exactly what a helicopter parent is, how to find your "Aha" moment, and take a simple test to determine if you are a heli-parent or not. We'll ask what kids think, because after all, don't you want to know their thoughts on the subject too? We will look at our national sport passions and how they impact our hovering ways. We'll see why former professional athletes' kids end up playing in the pros and why their odds are so much better. We'll review the pursuit of college sports, the fiction and the reality.

We'll examine the perils of the parent coach, the toughest job in youth sports. We will look at a "behaviour change" model and apply the principles to controlling your own helicopter behaviours. We will decide together, what you should and shouldn't do so you can fully enjoy the sports experience with your kids. Finally, we will work with Twelve Steps to help get you on your way out of the Hovering Game.

Aren't you a bit curious as to where our parental hovering behaviour came from? Let's start from the beginning, with our own parents.

Chapter 1

Yesterday vs. Today

"When I was your age, I walked five miles to school, each way!"

BABY BOOMERS & TODAY'S KIDS

IT'S INEVITABLE THAT WE, AS PARENTS, LOOK BACK AT WHAT WE DID WHEN WE WERE kids and how we had it so much tougher. Much like the stories we heard from our parents (and grandparents), we like to compare our history to their reality. However, more often than not, there are lessons we learned from our parents, and lessons our kids can learn from us.

As a baby boomer kid, I grew up during the 1960s and '70s. I was born and raised in Winnipeg, Manitoba, a medium-sized city by North American standards. It was a typical city with business fare downtown surrounded by suburban sprawl. We lived in a middle class neighbourhood. The streets were straight and parallel, four blocks to a mile, boulevards on both sides of the street, lined with young trees. In those days, fathers in our community had jobs working long hours and their spouses were often stay-at-home moms.

Our parents (as most next generation parents do) wanted a better life for their kids than they had (as their parents did), so staying in school and getting good grades was paramount. Sound familiar? However, back then, few parents had a university, or even a high school education, so while they knew it was a good idea to go to college, they didn't really know how to help us get there. My parents used to say "get good grades in school so you can go to university and become a professional," (which to them meant a doctor or a lawyer). Anything short of that was failure in my parents' eyes.

Today, much has changed. Educated beyond just high school and undergraduate degrees, today's parents not only want their children to become professionals like the "old days" but they think they have the knowledge to assist them with getting there. What kids learn in school today is far more advanced than when their parents were in school. The question is, are their parents qualified to help them with the advanced levels of math and sciences? More importantly, kids today have less of an opportunity to learn by themselves because many parents keep holding their hands in all aspects of their lives.

When it came to leisure time, we were for the most part, left to our own devices, occupying our spare time outside playing around the neighbourhood. Outdoor activities (which was always preferable) either meant street games like tag, kick the can, hide and seek or some pick-up sports game like hockey, football or baseball. When the weather wasn't cooperating, we would find things to do inside. There was television, but we were limited to only two or three stations (and no colour TV until I was twelve or so). So with few channel choices, we would opt to create our own games to keep us busy. In essence, less was done *for* kids and more was done *by* kids.

In those days, we were far more independent, with parents allowing kids to do what they wanted on their own (as long as they were home in time for dinner). When I was thirteen, my two younger brothers (twelve and nine) and I, would catch the 6:30 a.m. bus on the weekends to the downtown city bus depot (on Main Street, not the safest place), then hop on a Greyhound, and ride forty-five minutes out of town to Lockport, a popular fishing destination. With fishing gear in tow, we would spend the day casting on the river, and return home with a few fish for our mother to fry up for dinner. Today, if three boys under the age of thirteen in our community did something like that, the parents would likely be reported and charged with child abandonment or endangerment.

When it came to organized sport, parents would rarely attend their kids' games as spectators. Most parents were fans of professional sports, not unlike today, but chose to let the kids play without attendance or moral support. Most of the time we would walk to the local rink, field or community centre, with gear in hand, rain or shine, snow or wind. If we were lucky enough to get a ride from dad, he would just drop us off and after practices or games we would make our way back home on our own. Teams were coached by those rare dads who knew something about sports and often would be found coaching multiple sports teams all year round.

As a kid, I loved sports. I played all of the community-based team sports up until junior high school, and then played school sports through to university. There wasn't a sport, whether team or individual that I wouldn't or didn't try. I loved to play and compete. At the time, I didn't remember feeling a loss by not having my parents around to cheer me on. I just loved to play. But somewhere in the course of becoming a parent, I found myself wishing my mom and dad would have been there to support me, particularly when I played high school sports. I was determined not to let that happen to my kids.

Was that a noble thought? Maybe, but this common theme of participating in every part of your child's life is what spawned the helicopter dilemma.

FOCUS FEEDBACK FROM PARENTS

IN FOCUS GROUPS CONDUCTED WITH PARENTS WHO HAVE CHILDREN IN YOUTH sports, I asked questions about their own childhood and sports. Most had memories of their parents not supporting them in the stands and feeling it would have been nice if they could have been there. Their parents' attitude created the same notion that I had, "I am going to be there for my kid."

There were some parents I interviewed whose own parents did watch them play. They were the only parents cheering them on in the stands. These parents remember this being a great experience and they too have reciprocated with the notion of support like they had. They loved having their parents there.

A supportive parent spectator is one of the seeds that give rise to helicopter parenting. Driving kids to practice, watching those practices and spectating at games is part of today's norm for child rearing, which can be and often is a good thing. But bring in the overly obstructive parent and things get ugly. In my day, when the basketball team was playing a home game, the stands would be full—of kids from the school. Rarely would you see a parent in the stands. Today, most of the spectators are parents, grandparents, aunts and uncles of all the players.

WHY DO WE WATCH OUR KIDS PLAY?

IT IS IMPORTANT TO UNDERSTAND WHERE WE CAME FROM, WHERE WE ARE NOW, and where we are going. Parents today have careers (vs. jobs), and they value their downtime with their children. If you are a high-participation parent, actively involved in all of your child's sporting endeavours, complete this simple multiple choice question exercise:

Why do I attend my child's sporting activities?

A) To cheer on and support my child.

B) Because my child wants me to be there.

C) To watch over my child to make sure he or she is not hurt physically or emotionally.

D) To supervise and observe the coaches and how they coach my child.

E) Because I love to watch the game and watch my child play.

F) To relive my sporting dreams and aspirations through my child's play.

G) Because I need to be in control of my child's play.

H) So I can give my child advice and feedback on how to play the game.

Now follow the instructions below:

1. Answer the questions as truthfully as you can.
2. Choose ALL of the answers above that apply.
3. Rank your choices in order, from most to least applicable.
4. Now go through the same exercise, answering the questions for your spouse.
5. Get your spouse to go through the exercise themselves and then for you as well.
6. Now compare your answers.

Going through this exercise could be the start of awareness that helicopter parenting may exist within you.

FIRST FAST FIVE

I ALWAYS FIND IT EASIER TO REMEMBER THINGS I'VE READ BY SUMMARIZING them using key points. It's a quick synopsis of what was said, put in a slightly different way. If you don't catch the point during the chapter, recap with the Fast Fives. Here is the first of many Fast Fives.

FAST FIVE

- Think back about why YOU had fun participating in sports as a kid.
- Learn from your own past to help shape the future of your children.
- Acknowledge how things have changed, and how things are still the same.
- Bask in the glory of your childhood and share your experience with your children.
- Actively participate in your child's activities for the right reasons.

"We all, as parents, are laughing at ourselves and helicopter parenting and saying, 'This isn't the way we were parented; we were allowed to run free.' When I talk to my friends, we are all fascinated by what we are doing, but we can't seem to stop ourselves."

—Liane Moriarty, Australian Author

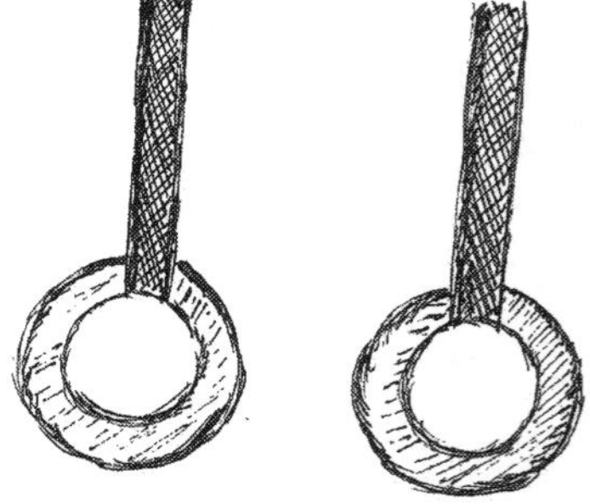

Chapter 2

Youth Sport: Our Continental Landscape

"Physical fitness is not only one of the most important keys to a healthy body, it is the basis of dynamic and creative intellectual activity."

—John F. Kennedy, 35th President of the United States

WHY DO KIDS PLAY SPORTS?

WHY DO KIDS DO IT? WHY DO THEY PARTICIPATE IN SPORTS? IS IT AN INNER DESIRE to just play; is it a force driven by their parents, or a combination of both? Many answers come to mind. First let's look at some background facts about kids sports in Canada and the US.

To start, be it known to all that participation in youth sports is on the decline. It is estimated (but difficult to quantify) that over 30 million kids between the ages of five and seventeen play some sort of organized sport in the US and Canada.[1] However, the numbers have been steadily decreasing, and while there are numerous reasons (including birth rates and socio-economics which are somewhat uncontrollable) much of the conventional wisdom (and common popular thought) could be attributed to the very popular statistic "70% of kids participating in organized sport drop out after 13 years of age." However, according to a study completed by the Sports & Fitness Industry Association, more kids than ever are not participating in organized sport. In the past five years, overall participation has dropped by 44%. A

[1] **Bruce Kelley,** *"Hey, data data – swing!"*, 2013

particularly disconcerting finding was that less than one in three children between the ages of six and twelve participated in fitness activities three times a week. Most of the major sports have been affected.[2]

However, some sports including rugby, beach volleyball, lacrosse and gymnastics have actually been able to buck the trend. A combination of an increase in popularity worldwide and/or a change of pace for parents and kids looking for something different to do are the main reasons why. This means that the mainstream sports have in fact declined even further.

Another sport that has seen a reverse trend for the better is hockey in the US. USA Hockey and the US Olympic Committee (who were dealing with decreased participation in their numbers) have been working hard to reverse their declining stats. However, with recent changes including reduced travel, safety rule changes, broader accessibility and encouragement of their athletes to play other sports, they have seen a recent increase in player participation.[3]

Could it be that beyond issues like population decline, sedentary distractions (computer and video games), fear of injury, cost of participation and de-emphasis on specialization at an early age, that over-parenting could be part of the reason for the decline as well? Almost certainly. Easy to say, hard to prove. But it's out there.

FIRST WORLD STRATEGIES

Regardless of the reasons, first world countries, including Canada and the US, have identified a decline in physical activity as a serious problem for the future health of their populations, and are doing something about it.

Developed countries are very aware of the sedentary distractions and the inactivity problems they create in today's society. The decline of physical activity in their populations and the effects this has on the health and well-being of their people has become a worldwide problem. Many of these countries have put more emphasis on financial support to develop physical infrastructure and information awareness campaigns primarily targeting youth. The strategy is to positively impact physical

[2] **SFIA**, *Sports, Fitness, and Leisure Activities Topline Participation Report*, 2016

[3] **USA Hockey**, *Membership Stats*, 2015

activity, to increase participation in organized sport, active transportation (walking or biking to destinations), active play (non-organized activities) and decreasing modern sedentary behaviours (like computer play).

Another point to consider is the differences in organized sport systems throughout the first world. How do the youth sport systems in our two North American nations differ from the rest?

North American youth sport is quite different from the majority of the first world countries. In Canada and the US, youth participation in organized sport happens through the school system, community centre and club programs.

By contrast, in most other developed nations, youth sport is supported exclusively through a sports club system. Kids start at a very early age in whatever sport their parents put them into and they participate at the club level all the way through to adulthood, leading them in some rare cases to a professional sports career. These clubs are often affiliated with a professional team based in the club so young athletes can aspire to become a pro. Conversely, aspirations to play pro in North America filter through the college and university sports systems.

Which system is better? It is debatable, but I find it particularly amusing to speak with those involved in each system. Both will cite the other's problems and say they have the better sports structure. Understanding these vastly different approaches to sports can only help in the long-term evolution of youth sports on a global scale.

DIVERSITY & PURSUIT

Has anything changed in the way Canada and the US supports youth sports over the years? Plenty can be discussed, but I believe there have been two major shifts over the past few decades that are relevant to the Hovering Game: The increased diversity of sport opportunities for youth, and parents' pursuit of excellence for their kids within the diversity of those opportunities.

Diversity of Choice: I like to classify youth sports in North America as either early adoption or intermediate adoption sport activities. Early adoption means organized sport kids start playing at age five to twelve. Intermediate adoption refers to organized sport that kids begin playing at age thirteen and up.

Early adoption team sports in North America include baseball, football, basketball, soccer and hockey. Individual early adoption sports include tennis, gymnastics, swimming and figure skating to name a few. Parents who want their kids to reap the benefits of being involved in sports start them at the early adoption age of around five years old. The parents' primary intent is to get their child involved in an activity that is fun and invigorating. They often choose to initially enrol their kids in the individual sports for things like motor skill acquisition (and for fun, right?). For team sports, parents register their kids to give them their first team experience, and competition of course in both individual and team sports cases.

By age twelve or so, kids have been playing these early adoption sports for around seven years. If they have been in the sport for this long, the kids and parents have been exposed to the numerous additional opportunities (and pressure) to specialize. More practices, more games, more off-season training, more time, more money, just more. Not all succumb to the community pressure and opt instead to try something different for their child.

These new options are made available partly through exposure to new sports in junior high school. The intermediate adoption sports abound, including team sports like volleyball, rugby and lacrosse. Individual sports include track and field, golf, martial arts and numerous x-game sports. Further, with coverage of the Olympics and other sporting events on television, kids are exposed to every sport you can imagine. The growth of these sports usually spikes when their country wins a medal in an Olympic cycle, especially the intermediate adoption sports. You can't find any sport in the world that doesn't have a Canadian or American association that offers youth programs. The diversity and opportunities today are enormous.

Pursuit of Excellence: Conventional wisdom would suggest that parents' obsession with the pursuit of excellence for their kids in sports has gotten progressively worse. If this is true, why?

Think about this: An international study was conducted in 2014 by Active Healthy Kids Canada (AHKC), and supported by ParticipACTION, on physical activity for children and youth. This study compared data from fifteen countries (including Canada and the US) on a wide scope of topics, one of which included active transportation.[4] Active transportation refers to how the child gets to where they want to go. How they get to school, or social, sports and other activities. Are they driven? Do they walk or bike? Do they take the bus?

[4] **Active Healthy Kids Canada,** *Report Card on Physical Activity for Children and Youth*, 2014

In Canada, only 24% of kids between the ages of five and seventeen walk, bike or take another form of active transportation vs. being driven or taking the bus to school. In the US, the percentage is even less. This is part of our society's new behaviour—we drive our kids everywhere for many reasons, not least because safety is important for our children, time is precious and it's quicker, and driving is part of our community culture.

If you drive your kid to practice or a game, do you drop them off then pick them up, or do you stay and watch? More parents stay than ever before. (Think of the questions in Chapter 1, how many parents are spectators? Is every child represented in the stands by a parent or two?) This continual participation is one of the contributing factors to bringing out the inner helicopter parent. When parents attend practices and games, other parents can influence their thoughts about their child's pursuit of excellence. Why is Johnny doing better than my son? Should I get my son some extra training or coaching like Johnny has?

THE NEW SPORT PARADOX

IN YOUTH SPORT, IT IS COMMON FOR PARENTS TO MOVE THEIR KIDS FROM ONE sport to the next, for numerous reasons. They aren't having fun anymore, there are physical limitations, geographic, economic and more. In moving to a new sport, there are some challenges that may not be as obvious as you may think.

I have been running a sport organization (volleyball, an intermediate adoption sport) for the past thirteen years. I have seen and been through a lot. When the teams in our club are selected, I speak to each of the parents by age group about many things, our "parent code of conduct" among them. What I have noticed over the years is this:

Parents who have their kids in early adoption sports are used to the dog-eat-dog, highly competitive nature of those sports. Their kids have already been playing for up to seven years. With the rep teams in those sports, kids are expected to put in extra time, play year-round and be fully committed already to their early adoption sport. Parents are surprised and revitalized when they hear about our club's philosophy regarding parental behaviour. As a club, we *do* encourage kids to play multi-sport. We also *do not* encourage parental hovering. But they do it anyway.

Most helicopter parents in intermediate adoption sports come from the early adoption group who already show signs of parental hovering behaviours. But this behaviour can also be seen with new parents to youth sport. These are parents who, for whatever reason, have had their kids involved in other activities like dance, music and fine arts. If they haven't involved their kids in sports before, they either go in one of two directions. They either stay the course of "sports are for fun" or get influenced by heli-parents who bring out the worst in them, like others before them.

THE BENEFITS OF YOUTH SPORT

YOUTH SPORT IS A GOOD THING, RIGHT? I STRONGLY BELIEVE IT IS. WHY IS SPORT so important for today's youth? Many studies and articles have been written on the subject, and certainly parents with a sport background are all too aware of the benefits. Here is my list of the Top Ten benefits of youth sport (in no particular order):

1. Sport promotes learning new skills while having fun.
2. Sport contributes to social interaction with friends.
3. Sport participation improves and develops self-esteem.
4. Sport keeps kids out of trouble.
5. Sport increases focus, concentration and academic performance at school.
6. Sport stimulates healthy growth and development of physical literacy.
7. Sport contributes to stronger bones, muscles and joints.
8. Sport improves posture and balance.
9. Sport strengthens the heart muscle.
10. Sport maintains a healthier weight range.

ORGANIZED VS. UNORGANIZED ACTIVITIES

ORGANIZED SPORT IS A GOOD THING, AND NEEDED IN TODAY'S STRUCTURED -parenting society. But we have become overly dependent on it and our kids are not indulging in unplanned, unsupervised play enough. In the AHKC study, kids were found to only spend four hours a week in unorganized active play. Kids benefit from natural unplanned physical activity and the diverse way it offers to enhance their social skills.

ASK YOURSELF THIS QUESTION:

WHAT KINDS OF PHYSICAL AND NON-PHYSICAL ACTIVITIES DOES MY CHILD PARTICIPATE IN?

A) **Organized sport** – team or individual sports.
B) **Scheduled family leisure activities** – hiking, camping, water and winter sports.
C) **Unorganized group activities** – play time with friends and family.
D) **Sedentary activities** – TV, video games, puzzles and family games.
E) **Other non-sport activities** – art, reading and make-believe.

Rank these activities twice. Once from the most to least important to you as a parent, and again with most to least quality time your child spends participating in each. How do they compare? Is this what you expected?

Now ask yourself this question: When was the last time you played or joined in with your child in one of these activities? I am sure you go to your son or daughter's game, but how frequently do you "play" together?

If it's been awhile, consider re-engagement with your child. Being a physically active role model for your child has numerous benefits. You'll be pleased that you did and so will your kid!

FAST FIVE

- Kids' sports are good.
- Consider increasing your child's active transportation activity.
- Diverse options exist; don't specialize too early, what's the rush?
- Find a good reason to pursue excellence for your kids in sports.
- Play something, anything, anytime, anywhere, with your children.

> "Intelligence and skill can only function
> at the peak of their capacity
> when the body is healthy and strong."
>
> —*John F. Kennedy, 35th President of the United States*

Chapter 3

What's All This Fuss About Helicopter Parenting Anyway?

"The more risks you allow children to take, the better they learn to take care of themselves."

—Roald Dahl, British Novelist

DEFINITION: HELICOPTER PARENTING

WHAT DOES "HELICOPTER PARENTING" MEAN? THERE ARE MANY DEFINITIONS OUT there, but I like this one best, sourced from the Oxford Dictionary: *"A parent who takes an overprotective or excessive interest in the life of their child."*

The term "helicopter parent" was first introduced in Dr. Haim Ginott's 1969 book (yes, 1969!) *Between Parent & Teenager* by teens who said their parents hovered over them like a helicopter.[5] The term became so popular that it was actually included as a dictionary entry in 2011.

What does it mean when a parent is described as a person as living vicariously through their children? The word *vicarious* is defined as "Felt or enjoyed through imagined participation in the experience of others."

When applying the word vicarious and the definition of a helicopter parent in the context of youth in sport, the hovering behaviour becomes clear. The parent who only achieved a certain level of success in their chosen sport, pushes their child

[5] **Haim G. Ginott,** *Between Parent & Teenager,* 1969

to the next level, whatever that may be, fulfilling some dream of their own, not their child's. Living vicariously through a child in someone's sport dream may in fact, be uncommon in practice. So it may be that the heli-parents in our society represent a small minority but are the loudest. However, I can say with certainty that most parents have helicopter thoughts at some point in their lives. When that thought takes hold and becomes an obsession, this is the essence of helicoptering.

Helicopter parents not only hover over their own children, but they end up affecting others, dusting up the ground, creating more heli-parents. This is the keeping up with the Jones's behaviour. The hovering parent is an incredibly dangerous influencer, whether they realize it or not.

SUPERHERO PARENTS

An exception to the helicopter-parenting rule is parents with special needs kids. These parents are the superheroes of our time. They are often misunderstood and unfairly judged by other parents in our society. People without any knowledge or experience can't possibly comprehend the reality of parenting kids with special needs and the daily circumstances, many challenging, that they are simply dealing with every day. Rarely are they helicoptering. If you notice one of these parents displaying what appear to be helicopter parenting behaviours, do not be deceived. They are doing their best. Do not judge them. Admire them. They are superhero parents.

THE HAVES AND HAVE-NOTS

Helicopter parenting behaviour can occur in any parent, whether it is in thought or in practice, but is it more dominant with middle and upper income parents? In my research I have spoken to those of all socio-economic backgrounds, including lower income parents as well as professionals working with less fortunate families.

Here are the results of my findings: If a parent grew up in a high-income family, they were usually well educated and now want the same for their kids. They see the economic challenges of today's world with higher housing, education and consumer product costs. They want the same for their child as they had, and better, of course. They helicopter to do more for their child to give them the advantage so they can maintain or improve on the lifestyle they grew up with. This becomes another seed for growing helicopter parenting behaviour.

Middle-income parents are a bit of a high-income personality hybrid. They definitely want an even better lifestyle for their kids compared to their own childhood. They see the vast benefit of youth sport, but are at risk of getting caught in the lift that is created in the Hovering Game by the helicopter pilots. I believe these parents are at the most risk of being influenced and demonstrate the most anxiety over whether to play the Hovering Game or not.

So where do the low-income families fit in? First and foremost, they simply do not have the same opportunities to be involved in sports as the other two classes primarily because they can't afford the costs associated with most organized sports. Their main concern in life is being able to afford basics like food and shelter. The last thing they are worried about is the pursuit of excellence in sports. Low-income parents have the same dreams for their kids, but can have a more realistic view of life's challenges and what is truly important. So do helicopter parenting behaviours exist at all with low-income parents?

I spoke to Daniel To, a Principal of Education Services in a major school district in BC. He just completed writing his thesis on "Parental Support for Students Who Participate in High School Athletics: An Exploration of the Perceived Involvement of Parents and Its Effect on Student Self-Efficacy and Academic Success." I asked him whether he thought low-income families are less susceptible to helicopter behaviours than the middle and high-income groups.

> *In my research I interviewed numerous student athletes whose families came from all backgrounds, low, medium and high income. The students from low income family schools had the same perceptions as those from high and middle income schools. Parents were equally as involved, regardless of the income status. I believe that there is an inherent risk, regardless of the socio-economics of any of them becoming a helicopter parent. Low-income parents may not have the luxury of being at the games or practices, but they still find other ways to hover. It is more of a behind the scenes approach to helicoptering; emails, phone calls, texts, they find a way to stay in touch, it still amounts to the same behaviour.*

All communities are populated with haves and have-nots, some more than others. But another dimension exists, the impact of immigration. Third generation North Americans (or older) have already seen the movie: "I'm going to watch my kids in their sports, because my parents didn't." However, new Canadians and Americans have not. Those who are first or second generation newbies carry the same values as our parents and grandparents. Some of them left a tough life in their former country, they know the value of education for children and they don't care much about sports. You don't often see a first generation immigrant parent watching their kids playing traditional North American sports.

However, as they become more North Americanized, they eventually become part of the community with cheers and support, which can and does lead to hovering behaviour. First and second generation parents demonstrate another form of helicopter parenting behaviour when their child is enrolled in the sport that *they* played as a child; their national sport. When a new North American from South America say, enrolls their son or daughter in soccer, all bets are off. This is a sport they know, understand and are hyper passionate about. Unfortunately, they are now as highly susceptible to helicopter behaviour as any other parent. Regardless of the background, all parents are capable of hovering. It just comes out in different ways for different people.

WHY ARE YOU A HELICOPTER PARENT?

HOW DOES THE HELICOPTER PARENTING "THOUGHT" TAKE HOLD OF US? WHY DO parents cross over from thought to practice? What are they afraid of? Why do they hover? Here are the most common reasons parents hover:

- **Over protection of the child** – taking control in an effort to protect them from harm.
- **Fear of failure** – fear of their child not succeeding and the impending consequences.
- **Overcompensation** – living through them vicariously.
- **Peer pressure from the parental community** – "I'm not doing enough", the perception of being a bad parent.
- **Falling behind** – Fear of other children getting an advantage and staying ahead of their own child.

Helicopter parents are anxious about their kid's welfare and success. They are obsessed with protecting their child from failure and disappointment. They provide excessive guidance and direction. They are more involved with their child's day-to-day activities than the average parent. They feel the need to "keep up with Jones's" to keep their child competitive. Essentially helicopter parents micro-manage their child's life.

> A low grade, not making the team, or not getting a certain job can appear disastrous to a parent, especially if it seems it could be avoided with parental involvement. But, many of the consequences [parents] are trying to prevent—unhappiness, struggle, not excelling, working hard, no guaranteed results—are great teachers for kids and not actually life-threatening. It just feels that way.
>
> *—Deborah Gilboa, M.D., AskDoctorG.com*

Part of the problem is that today our expectations from sport for our kids are more adult-goal oriented than child oriented. It's not about having fun, it's about the pot of gold at the end of the rainbow.

Helicopter parenting can start at an early age and continue through high school and university. Heli-parents can't stop hovering, and continue to be involved, often completing tasks that the child can do on their own.

Michael played basketball in grade twelve and was the star of his team. The team was competitive, finishing in the top three in the city league. They were knocked out of the championship round in the semi-finals. Michael was a great player in school, but not quite good enough to make a university basketball team. No big deal, he had his sights on a degree in business and he eventually became a successful accountant. Michael continued to play basketball in a men's league to have fun and stay in shape. He got married and had two boys. Michael is a tall man. His sons, according to many of his friends, will be taller than his 6'4" stature—tall enough to make it to the college varsity ranks for sure. He enrolled the boys in a basketball program for seven-year-olds and they looked very good out there. People started telling him, "Hey your sons have talent." Soon Michael started to dream of them making it as college basketball stars, and maybe even the NBA. His attitude towards his involvement and parenting changed. He became obsessed with them winning and started to give them regular coaching advice before, during (from the stands) and after games.

Michael fell into the initial trap of living vicariously through his two boys in basketball. Sparked by his own inability to reach his dream, he started to live his dream through his kids, and listening to parent advocates encouraged this. But isn't it supposed to be the kids' dream, not his?

During the parent focus group meetings I conducted, I never ever heard a parent admit that they were a heli-parent when asked the initial question, "are you a helicopter parent?" Be it pride, denial, or obliviousness, it wasn't until we got deeper into the discussion when parents starting coming clean with admission, and a sense of recognition, that maybe, just maybe, they had or did display parental hovering behaviour.

CONSEQUENCES

HELICOPTER PARENTS ARE FUELLED BY GOOD INTENTIONS. THEIR NATURAL parental instincts tell them to support and protect their kids in the best way they know how. But there are consequences to parental hovering and how it impacts their child's future behaviour. According to Kate Bayless in her article on Parents.com, there are some long-term consequences to helicoptering:[6]

Lost confidence and low self-esteem – Overindulgence can result in kids thinking that their parents don't trust them enough to do things by themselves, which can lead to a lack of self-confidence.

Poor coping skills – If the parent is always there to clean up a child's mess or prevent the problem from occurring in the first place, how will the child ever learn to cope with loss, disappointment, or failure? Helicopter parenting can make children feel less competent in dealing with the stresses of life on their own.

Low resilience – Kids lose their ability to adapt when parents hover excessively. They can never do things on their own because they have always been done for them in the past. Allowing kids to make mistakes and learn from them makes them stronger, tougher and more resilient. Covering for them all the time results in an inability to handle unexpected change.

[6] **Kate Bayless,** *What is Helicopter Parenting?*, 2013

Undeveloped life skills – Parents who always answer the coach's emails, pack lunches, launder uniforms, and monitor their kids' progress in their sport (for them), even after their child is mentally and physically capable of doing these tasks, prevent their children from grasping these skills themselves. Driving your child to a job interview is one thing, but thinking it's okay to sit in on the interview is not, and will never teach them anything. So, do you really need to be in the middle of a discussion between your daughter and her fast pitch coach? Don't you see the harm?

Entitlement – Kids who have always had their social, academic, and athletic lives regulated by their parents to best fit their needs can become used to always having their way and thus they develop a sense of entitlement. When the kid who has always been a starter on the basketball team, now has to sit on the bench like all the other first year players, they can't handle it!

Anxiety – When a kid makes a mistake on the field, don't you think they know it? First, they recognize the mistake themselves. Then they hear from their teammates. Then the coach tells them. They have already heard it from multiple sources. On the way home, the parent tells them again what they already know. Imagine the anticipation of anxiety they feel when they know they are going to get bombarded repeatedly with criticism. Anxiety can lead to further behavioural and emotional issues including depression.

When I first started interviewing kids in the focus groups, I was secretly hoping that it wasn't as bad as I thought it was. And in fact, there were some who have never felt their parents were helicoptering. But most had stories to tell, some with discomfort about how their parents had either been or were currently playing the parental Hovering Game.

It's hard to admit that we are doing something wrong with our parenting. Sometimes, we just need to have our eyes opened. So ask yourself this question:

Am I a youth sport helicopter parent?

Has this made you think about your current parental behaviour towards your children in their sport activity? Maybe your spouse or a friend?

THE HOVER TEST

STILL UNSURE IF YOU ARE A HELICOPTER PARENT, OR IF SOMEONE CLOSE TO YOU IS? Then do yourself and family a favour and take the Hover Test. Answer these questions Yes or No for yourself, your spouse or a friend:

1. Do you lobby the coaches and administrators prior to or during tryouts for your son or daughter to ensure they have the best chance of making the team or program?
2. When you take your son or daughter to practice, do you stay and watch?
3. On the way home from the game, do you provide technical feedback to your son or daughter on how they played the game?
4. Do you keep track of your son or daughter's play time on the court, field or ice during a game compared to others on the team? Do you track the time the coach spends with your son or daughter during their training sessions?
5. Do you compare your son or daughter's abilities to others on the team and share these comparisons with other parents?
6. Do you "signal" or shout out instructions to your son or daughter during a game, competition or at practice on what to do or how to do it?
7. Do you intervene on behalf of your son or daughter about any team issues that have affected them with their coaches?
8. Do you pull your child off of a team or out of a program because you don't think it's competitive enough and you haven't asked your child what they want?

Scoring: If you have answered, "Yes" to any or all of these, then simply put, you are showing the behaviours symptomatic of a helicopter parent. Now, some of these questions apply more to parents with older kids, but starting to act this way can impact your child, even at a younger age.

In the next chapter, we will determine if and when you have had an "Aha" moment in the Hovering Game.

FAST FIVE

- Helicopter parenting has been around since the '60s.
- Every parent has had at the very least a thought that could be defined as helicoptering behaviour.
- Helicoptering robs the child of learning through making mistakes on his or her own.
- Any kind of unnecessary intervention in your child's athletic endeavours is considered helicopter parenting behaviour.
- Consider what it will take for you to overcome the fears that manifest themselves in helicopter parenting.

"You wouldn't worry so much about what others think of you if you realized how seldom they do."

—Eleanor Roosevelt, former First Lady

Chapter 4

The "Aha" Moment

"A moment of sudden insight or discovery."

—*Oxford Dictionary*

OH, I'M ONE OF *THOSE* PARENTS!

When my son was nine years old, he had been playing minor hockey for a few years. I can safely say that our parental community considered my wife and me to be "good" hockey parents. We drove him to practice (early mornings mostly), games and tournaments. We participated in the fundraisers, travelled to all home and away games. We sat/stood in the stands during the games with the rest of the parents and got along with the faithful quite well.

As often is in a game, our team parents on one side and the visitors' team's parents are on the other. Keep in mind that hockey is Canada's sport religion. As a Canadian you can't help but get wrapped up in it, no matter what level.

So the game is close, and there is (what I deemed to be) an illegal check at the other end of the ice (which I can barely see) against one of our players. The whistle is blown, but no penalty ensued. My Canadian cultural, animal instincts instantly take over, and I yell out in earnest "where's the call?"

An innocent comment (so I thought), but as many veteran rink rats know, sound travels well when the play is stopped. All of a sudden, I see the entire fan group in the stands of the visiting team lean over in unison and look towards me with a distinct look that says, "Oh, there's another one of those crazy hockey parents."

I cower back down on the bench seats and say to myself, wow, was that really me? Am I one of those parents? It made me feel awful. Why did I yell out my thoughts? What was I thinking? What must my son think of me? It was an instinctive reaction. But the consequences can impact your kid in so many ways.

Ironically, my son never thought anything of it, and he didn't even know it happened. But for me it was my "Aha" moment. Maybe I wasn't demonstrating the stereotypical heli-parenting traits at all. Maybe I was just an overzealous fan. But I did not want to be one of those parents. From that point on, I counted to ten before I said anything, and it became the start of how I wanted to behave and lead my children when it came to raising them as good sport citizens. Through this experience, I gained a heightened awareness of how to avoid becoming a helicopter parent.

WHAT IS AN "AHA" MOMENT?

AN "AHA" MOMENT IS A KNOCK ON THE HEAD, A FLASH OF LIGHT, A BUCKET OF water in the face. It's when you realize that what you said or what you did was out of character, or out of the character you want to be when raising your children.

In the focus group sessions with parents, the question was asked, "Have you ever had an 'Aha' moment?" Most would initially respond with a "no", almost as if to say, "I am not like that, that's not me." But as the sessions progressed and we revisited the question, the remaining naysayers would come back with a story that revealed some level of helicopter parenting. Sometimes one spouse would remind the other of a time that should have been an "Aha" moment for them. This is when the awareness factor sets in. I have yet to speak with any parents who have not had an "Aha" moment when it comes to parenting their child. The longer they think about it, the clearer the reveal.

AN "AHA" MOMENT CAN REVEAL ITSELF TO YOU IN A VARIETY OF WAYS:

- You recognize your own bad behaviour.
- Your spouse tries to tell you in many ways until there is a breakthrough.
- Your child snaps at you in a way that says, you're being a heli-parent.
- You notice a change in your child, one that is not positive, and sense it might be you that has affected this behaviour.
- You have a friend, colleague, team parent, coach, teacher or family member who confronts you with your behaviour.
- You recognize the behaviour in someone else, and realize you behave this way too.
- You attend a talk, read a book or article on the subject and the light just turns on.

FIND YOUR "AHA" MOMENT

HAVING AN "AHA" MOMENT IS A GOOD THING. IT'S WHEN A PARENT RECOGNIZES that their behaviour is bad. If you are able to realize that you have said or done something that represents bad behaviour either for the first time, or that you have been doing it all along, you are on the road to repair. If you act early enough, before your kids have been impacted for too long, the change for the better will have a long-lasting effect on their lives in a positive way.

Clayton was a leading NCAA National Tae Kwon Do competitor in his college days. He was a top athlete in his weight class. Competitive enough to be an Olympic athlete. But in the end he chose a different path. When he became a father of three boys, he enrolled them in Tae Kwon Do classes, all at an early age. By the time they had all reached about fourteen years old, they had dropped out and moved on from the sport. Clayton assumed that they stopped because they were bored, and they wanted to do something else. The something else was a non-sport, sedentary activity like video and computer games.

When the boys were older, in high school, he was driving two of them home one day and noticed some kids running cross country, training at the nearby track. Clayton said to the boys, "Isn't it great to see those kids still involved with sports? It's such a good thing, don't you think?" The boys didn't respond. Remembering that none of his boys were involved in sports anymore, and not sure why, he asked, "Why did you guys stop doing Tae Kwon Do anyway?" Both boys immediately responded, "Dad, you were always ragging on us, always pushing, we weren't having fun anymore." Clayton had his "Aha" moment, unfortunately too late in some ways, but just in time for another. He readily apologized to them, recognizing his mistake.

That was a big step for Clayton, to take responsibility for his actions with his children. He now knows that he needs to reassess how he can motivate and support his kids in their endeavours without over-parenting.

Consider yourself a lucky parent if you find out from your child that the hovering behaviours are taking their toll on your relationship while they are still in sports. You have the opportunity to change your behaviour. Clayton was one of the lucky ones. There are numerous stories out there about parents who took it to the extreme, didn't recognize the "Aha" moments and are now paying for it with a zero relationship with their kid.

In Chapter 11 we will discuss dos and don'ts. The don'ts represent bad behaviour. If you exercise any of the bad behavioural traits or actions, they are all "Aha" moments.

Ask yourself, have I ever said or done any of these don'ts? Recall the exact moment when. The one that really stands out. If you can't think of one, ask your spouse or close friend if they can recall any moment when you emulated those actions, and you will find your "Aha" moment. It's what you do with it that will determine your future relationship with your child.

FAST FIVE

- Think about how your child reacts to your comments or actions in their sport activities.
- Try to recall your "Aha" moment.
- Have you ever been confronted by others with hovering behaviour tendencies?
- Consider what you need to do to avoid an "Aha" moment with your child.
- Having an "Aha" moment is truly a good thing—it can be invigorating!

"Everybody is a genius. But if you judge a fish by its ability to climb a tree, it will live its whole life believing that it is stupid."

Albert Einstein, Physicist

Chapter 5

What Do the Kids Think?

"When I was a boy of fourteen, my father was so ignorant I could hardly stand to have the old man around. But when I got to be twenty-one, I was astonished at how much the old man had learned in seven years."

—Mark Twain, American Novelist & Humourist

A SOCCER STORY

I was watching one of my middle daughter's seven-year-olds soccer games. Her team was competitive, it wasn't rep, but the team was good. They were playing against a rival team. I guess the community would be considered small, because everyone seemed to know, or know of everyone else—everyone meaning the parents of course. Plenty of parents on both sidelines were cheering on their girls.

Midway through the game, there was a questionable non-call on the field. Now at seven years of age, who cares, but for some reason, one father did. He was so upset with the non-call, that when the next side-out whistle was blown, he sauntered over to the referee to have a "discussion" with him about it in the middle of the game.

The referee was a forty-something man, who in my opinion knew his stuff. But the conversation got heated and the father ended up pushing him before we knew what had happened. Parents and coaches from both sides were ready to step in, as chaos was about to ensue.

While this was all happening the father's daughter was within twenty paces of the confrontation. When the father pushed the referee, his daughter screamed out at the top of her lungs "DAAAADDDYYY!!!" and started to cry. The outbreak seemed to stop everyone in their tracks. The dad ran out to his daughter to calm her down. Cooler heads prevailed, the father did the best he could to apologize to her, but the damage was done. These things happen, still.

ACCORDING TO KIDS: WHY DO THEY PLAY SPORTS?

In Chapter 2, I asked the question, why do kids participate in sports? But what do the kids think? In a Michigan State University study conducted by the Institute for the Study of Youth Sports,[7] they asked boys and girls aged ten to twelve why they played sports. Here are the top five reasons they gave:

1. To have fun.
2. To do something I'm good at.
3. To improve my skills.
4. To stay in shape.
5. To get exercise.

"Winning" didn't even make the top-ten list. And these results are similar no matter where you look or what age they are. Kids play sports primarily because it's fun. This differs greatly from the many parents and coaches who are focused on winning. Even with older age groups, most kids would rather play on a losing team

[7] **Martha Ewing and Vern Seefeldt,** *Institute for the Study of Youth Sports,* 1990

than sit on the bench of a winning one. But when the coach plays everyone evenly, they are criticized for not playing to win. Yet that's not necessarily what the kids want. This doesn't mean the kids don't value winning, they just prefer playing or having fun over winning.

When children are introduced to organized physical activity at a young age, parents get involved in some way, shape or form. Parent and tot swimming classes, umpiring at T-ball, bringing mid game orange slices for soccer, and of course, coaching.

Young kids are, for the most part, oblivious to the parent being around other than when they get the reward of a smile, a pat on the back or a joyous "congratulations" for a touchdown or a back handspring. They don't immediately recognize the over-parenting that takes hold when competitiveness starts creeping in. Children don't notice the hovering until they get older, in their teens, when they start questioning their parents' behaviour.

When parents get caught in the Hovering Game, they begin to promote a more competitive environment, which can become confrontational between the parent and child, especially in the teenage years. So how do the thirteen to eighteen-year-olds feel about their parents' ongoing involvement?

FOCUS GROUP FINDINGS FROM KIDS

HERE ARE SOME INTERESTING FINDINGS FROM THE FOCUS GROUPS CONDUCTED with youth ranging in age from thirteen to eighteen. The feedback relates to their parents' involvement in their sporting life.

WHAT THEY DO LIKE:

- **Fan Support** – Having their family there to cheer them on.
- **Limo Service** – Getting driven everywhere—practices, games and tournaments.
- **Feeding Time** – Being fed and nourished, before and during the game or practice.
- **Post-Game Celebrations** – Going for food or ice cream after a game.
- **Love** – Hugs & kisses.

What they don't like:

- **Mixed Messages** – Getting confused when their coaches and parents are giving them different messages about what to do in their sport.
- **Embarrassment** – Being targeted by teammates and friends as a "momma's boy" or "daddy's girl" when they are constantly being overprotected and supervised.
- **Underachievement** – Getting down when it seems like their performance is never good enough for their parents.
- **Lack of Trust** – Feeling like they can't do anything without their parents "holding their hands."

What they wish for:

- "I wish my mom would just let me play."
- "I wish my parents would let my coach be the coach."
- "I wish my dad would just talk about something else on our way home from a game."
- "I wish my parents wouldn't embarrass me so much at games, and stop yelling."
- "I wish my mom would let me sleep in the hotel room with the rest of my teammates on road trips instead of rooming with her all the time."
- "I wish my parents would just let me have fun."

ANDY MURRAY'S MOTHER

In an article written in *The Telegraph*, Judy Murray, mother of Andy Murray, top world ranked tennis player, was asked about parenting and kids in her sport of tennis.[8]

> *It's important to know why the child is playing, as it has to be because they love tennis, she says. "Sadly, you do get instances of parents who are living their dreams through their children. The parents didn't get as far as they wanted when they were playing, so they will try to get their kids to win the tournaments for them. At*

[8] **Mark Hodgkinson**, *"Nightmare Tennis Parents Who Don't Play Ball"*, 2008

> *the end of the day, it should all be about the kids. I'm always getting asked if I was a pushy parent. I'll admit I often had to push to make things happen but I never had to push my kids because they always wanted to play.*

Know your child. If you don't, get to know them. Find out what they want. Just ask them.

FAST FIVE

- Kids don't like it when parents hover excessively.
- Winning is never everything for kids.
- Kids play sports because it's fun.
- Kids do appreciate all of the support from their parents, and allowing them to play.
- Remember what it was like when you were a kid, apply this to the kids of today and find a compromise.

> "If you never did you should.
> These things are fun, and fun is good."
>
> *—Dr. Seuss*

Chapter 6

The Religion of Hockey

"What if kids pressured us like we pressured them? Relax, it's just a game."

—Hockey Canada TV Commercial

EVERY NATION HAS ITS SPORT RELIGION

I WAS COACHING AT AN INTERNATIONAL VOLLEYBALL COMPETITION, AND AFTER ONE of the matches I had a conversation with the Brazilian head coach. I asked him, what is Brazil's national sport? He promptly replied "Volleyball of course." "But what about soccer?" I asked. The coach replied, "Volleyball is our national sport, but in Brazil, soccer is our religion."

Every nation has its sport religion. It is the professional sport in that country that is the most watched and followed on television and other media. The following of professional sport is the most common influence that gets kids into the sport. For Canada, hockey is the sport religion, for the US it's football (or basketball, take your pick). Other countries have their obsessions too, and there are many different ones. In Japan it's baseball (and the US, it's the "national pastime"), in India it's cricket; in New Zealand, South Africa and Australia it's rugby, in Indonesia it's badminton and of course soccer is the "religion" all over South America, Asia, Europe and Africa. The following of professional sport, whatever it may be for your country, is your nation's obsession.

CANADIAN HOCKEY RELIGION

A TYPICAL CANADIAN, I GREW UP IN THE HOCKEY CULTURE, AND HAVE MUCH appreciated the parallels of our national sport religion with those of other countries. We have the same feelings in our guts about our favourite NHL team. Love to see them win, hate to see them lose. It stays with us for our entire life. If hockey is not your sport religion, just plug in your sport obsession to this chapter, it doesn't matter what the sport is, the same applies to them all.

WHEN YOU BECOME A CANADIAN HOCKEY PARENT FOR THE FIRST TIME, THREE THINGS BECOME OBVIOUS:

- **Everyone talks hockey** – Whether you are an ex-player at the major junior level, played organized hockey as a kid, or just a fan, once your son or daughter steps on the ice, hockey talk becomes part of the water cooler, Saturday night party or family dinner discussion. To not talk about it just seems foreign to a Canadian.
- **Winning becomes the measure of success** – You may be one of the few exceptions, but the majority of us measures their child's team's success by the win/loss column. Lots of people will "speak" development, but they will "think" winning.
- **Every kid is going to the NHL** – Of course not, but deep down, like every child in Canada that laces up a pair of skates, every parent of that child has the "dream" of making it. It is what keeps their passion and joy for the sport alive.

A HOCKEY STORY

IF YOU HAVE OR HAVE HAD A SON OR DAUGHTER IN MINOR HOCKEY, I EMPATHIZE. I have been there, with all of the ups and downs and the unrealistic pressures that surround the game. Every parent has stories to tell about their minor hockey experiences. These experiences are part of the Hovering Game culture, best shown through the religion of hockey. Here is my story.

> As parents, we didn't have any preconceived notions of what sport our kids would play. Both my wife and I have a volleyball background; we just knew that youth sport was good for us, and would

be good for our children. We had no idea what our kids would do, but sometimes things just happen by osmosis.

There was much to influence our son to play hockey. First, I am a pro sport fan by nature. I follow all sports, pro or amateur, and I am a Vancouver Canuck fan. My brother was a Vice President with the Canucks at the time, so we were uniquely exposed to the team and hockey personalities more often than the average fan.

At around four years old, we enrolled our son in power skating, just to see how it would go. He seemed to like it and he did okay out there. For our son's fifth birthday we bought him roller blades (which were popular in our neighbourhood in those days). Upon returning from work the next day, my son runs up to the car to tell me, "Hey dad, the kids on the street taught me how to roller blade today!" My dream to teach and see him skate on our roads was all but taken away from me by a couple of "street kids." Soon after, he was enrolled in ice hockey at the youngest age offered in our community. Our journey into the world of minor hockey began.

I was never much of a hockey player. I struggled with skating skills. But I loved the game with the stick and puck. My best memories are of walking to the outdoor rink near our house and playing pick-up with whoever was around. I loved to play any sport that was hockey-like. Street/ball hockey, floor hockey, even broomball, any neighbourhood game. So while I wasn't able to offer any coaching services to my son's hockey association, I was a fan.

Our son was one of those natural athletes—it seems no matter what sport they try, they were good at it. And he was a good hockey player, right up there with the best in his age group (which is important?). He played house, then rep hockey at the community level, representing our local municipality in the top league in his age group. We attended all the games, the 5:45 a.m. weekday practices, hot chocolate at Timmy's, the team bonding events, shake-the-can and pub night fundraisers, all of the other extracurricular activities that are associated with an organized team sport like hockey. We were "good" hockey parents.

With hockey being all around us in family, friends and of course our national sport, it was inevitable that our son (in his mind) was going to play in the NHL. He would say, "Dad, when I grow older, I am going to play for the Canucks!" Not, just the NHL, our home pro team! You never want to shatter your child's dreams, especially at a young age. But we knew the odds were extremely slim, so what's a dad to do?

As parents, we stayed fairly neutral, simply enjoying the dream with him, even though we knew it was unrealistic and way too early to consider. We would throw hints at him, that it may not be as easy as he thinks (like getting drafted by a team other than the Canucks). As our son got a bit older, he realized how the system worked and that it was less likely for him to make the Canucks, but he "would" make the NHL. As the years went on, he understood that for him to have a chance he would have to make a junior hockey team and take the necessary steps. By this time, he was around eleven. Eleven, and he is thinking about a career choice! Hockey religion, a powerful thing.

It seems easy to the average hockey parent (the one who has been watching the game all his life, and is of course, an expert) to pick out (at age ten) who is going to make it in the NHL, right? Part of the conversation that takes place at the rink when parents are watching, is about who is great, good and not so good. But when you are considering your child, parents have a tough time being objective.

We were very realistic in our expectations. We knew how small the odds were for our son to make it. We just weren't sure what all of the reasons were. There is something inside of you, part inner hockey passion, part parental bias that can lead you astray and get you thinking your son has a chance. It is most often fuelled by the few parents who tell you, "Hey, your son is very good, he could make it one day." When enough parents, coaches, friends and family come up to you over the course of the season, to tell you how good your son is, you can't help but to start thinking, well, maybe?

If you let this feeling take hold, then every time your son makes a good pass, scores a goal, makes a save or checks a player, you will see nothing but the great. You will ignore the mistakes (which are part of growing in any sport), and his shortcomings as a player.

Admittedly, we allowed ourselves fleeting thoughts surrounding his successes, but as coaches of other sports, we recognized the mistakes and weaknesses. We never let it take hold, but the dream would always be present, as would the risk of playing the Hovering Game. It's part of the hockey culture.

Between the ages of nine and twelve, our son played rep hockey with a certain level of success. He loved to play and couldn't get enough of it. He started playing spring hockey on a "travel" team. They are the ones that take the best rep hockey players from a few municipalities to compete in regional competitions. Our most memorable experience was at the Stampede Challenge, a huge summer hockey tournament in Calgary. What really stood out at the tournament was the size difference between kids. Some were well under 5', while a select few were as tall as 5'6". A twelve-inch difference in height can mean a lot in hockey. Luckily, there was no hitting at that age, yet. The boys had a great run and finished second in the tournament, playing teams from all over Canada. At the time, it felt like he was at the top of his game, and we were at the top of our enjoyment as parents.

The following year, I was asked to manage my son's rep hockey team. It seemed like a good idea at the time, so I agreed. Team managers have the best and worst of both worlds. You get to experience the inside workings of the league and see the game from the coach's perspective. You also see the ugly side of helicopter parenting in full flight. Our coach played some major junior as a kid and was a vice president with a mid-sized corporation. He knew how to manage people. He was also a no-nonsense guy who was difficult to read and hard to approach. Parents didn't feel comfortable questioning or challenging him, so they would often complain to me first. Did they really ever have anything to complain about? No! But it's part of the hockey culture. The hovering parent who thinks their son should be playing on a line with someone else, playing centre not defense or not getting enough ice time in games were the parents who would come to me first, hoping I could influence the coach. In the end, it was a good experience for me but being the manager really opened my eyes to the extreme helicopter parenting behaviours that exist in our national sport.

During my season as the team manager, I had to attend our local hockey association's AGM. The stage was set with the association directors, all sitting in front at a long table. The attending members (about 100) were sitting in chairs, opposite the executive, classroom style. One of the agenda items was a discussion about playtime and positions. It involved the direction of the association, specifically regarding the spirit of play and the importance of playing different roles on the ice.

When the executive members were finished with this topic, one of them asked the audience if there were any questions. A mother stood up and addressed the directorship. "My son is a centre iceman. That is the position he plays, and that is the position he is going to play on his team." One of the directors took the microphone and addressed the woman. "With all due respect, your son is eight years old! We do not condone specialization at eight years old, and you will not legislate the position your son plays. Now please sit down." Someone with integrity. Bravo!

For the most part, our team parents were great. But it's always the helicopter parent who likes to stir the pot or start the rebellion that creates problems for the rest. They are like John Belushi's character, John Blutarsky in *Animal House*, who gives the rousing speech in the frat house towards the end of the movie, finishing with "Who's with me!?" and runs out of the room. In the movie, no one follows him. Unfortunately, in hockey many do follow.

By the end of the season, our son started to complain a bit about his calves hurting. He was finding it difficult to push off to skate. Our son had become a smooth, fast skater, one of his best attributes, so it was a bit of a concern. After the season was over we took him to the doctor and he was diagnosed with acute Achilles tendinitis in both legs. We surmised that with him playing hockey for eleven months out of the year his tendons had become extremely tight and inflexible because of the limitations created by wearing skates (limited movement forward and back due to the ankle guard at the back). We decided to sit out spring hockey, rest up, rehab and try again at summer camp in August prior to rep tryouts in September.

The rest over the summer didn't seem to help. At the August camp, the tendinitis flared up again. September came, and with it, rep tryouts. One hour prior to the first tryouts, our son came down from his room and said, "I don't think I can play anymore. My legs still hurt. I can't keep skating as fast as I used to. I don't want to play if I can't help the team like I have done before."

We talked about it a bit more, but it was clear he couldn't do it. We told him that he would need to call his teammates and explain. About an hour after tryouts started, the phone calls came, from the parents. The news sent some shockwaves through the hockey community for sure. And the rumours started to flow, likely from the helicopter parents, who loved to stir that pot—he didn't like the coach, he had a heart condition and he didn't want to play anymore. It was amusing, yet at the same time ridiculous and somewhat disturbing to hear these untrue stories.

> I have to admit; we had mixed emotions about hockey being over for our son. On the one hand we were relieved. Hockey can be a health risk, with the speed of the game and unlike other team sports, a boundary with walls (boards). Your child is still just a kid. Your parental instincts tell you to protect them from harm.
>
> On the other hand, it felt like we were going through withdrawal. It had become part of our weekly ritual to be at the rink, watch the games and hang out with our friends. Just like that, it was over. But in the end, we (and he) got over it. He enrolled in community football and started playing high school sports (volleyball and basketball). He and we had finally moved on.

In retrospect, I learned some lessons from this whole experience as a hockey parent and how helicopter parenting manifests itself so easily in minor hockey in Canada.

DREAMS

I THINK ALLOWING YOUR KIDS TO HAVE DREAMS IS ALL PART OF THE PROCESS, regardless of whether you think the dream is realistic or not. Nothing offends me more than someone who shatters dreams. To dream big, to reach for the stars, is part of life. Dreams are what keep us alive. But when the parent takes over the dream from their child, it becomes dangerous.

In hockey culture, "the dream" of your kid making the NHL manifests itself like a cold virus. Someone gets it, and then gives it to everyone else. I like to classify three types of NHL dream hockey parents.

THE DREAMING PARENT WHO—

A) Truly believes their kid is going to make it in the NHL.

B) Says outwardly that their kid won't make it in the NHL, but inwardly believes it.

C) Says outwardly, and truly believes their kid won't make it in the NHL, but would love it if they did, and deep down, hope they will.

Those who are A's are the most dangerous, as they demonstrate some of the most common helicopter parenting traits. They are the ones who put their kids into extra "everything" at the earliest age and opportunity, convincing all others around them to do the same. These are the type of parents that create the most problems. These are the parents who lobby the parents of other kids who are (in their mind) not quite as good as their son, but, if they keep playing, their son will continue to stand out. They will insist that others participate in extra stuff, such as dry land training, spring hockey and summer camps. "If your son isn't doing any of these things, they will fall behind and not make the rep team next year."

B's are the most vulnerable to coercion by the A's. They are easily convinced. They are the followers, the ones who are part of the riot to oust the coach, the lobby to cut a weaker player from the team or excommunicate a less than participating parent. They are the sheep following the herd dog. The helicopter parent within them says if I follow the A's, one day our kid could make it. Kids dreams are okay, parents' dreams are the ones to worry about.

C parents pose the lowest risk of playing the Hovering Game. As parents, my wife and I were probably C's. C's stay true to their beliefs and convictions. Rightly so. They understand the high improbability of their son making it in the NHL. But C's are still susceptible to helicopter parenting behaviour. It happens when they continuously focus on what their kid does positively on the ice, ignoring any other realistic perspective. Sometimes it's hard not to ignore. Their dreams are further magnified when people (A's and B's) tell them how great their kid is. As long as they keep it real, things turn out okay, resulting in minimal hovering behaviour.

OF THE WORST BEHAVIOUR

ANY NATIONAL SPORT RELIGION CAN BRING OUT THE ABSOLUTE WORST IN PEOPLE. As Canadians, we are bombarded with negative stories in the press about the psycho parent who punches out a referee or the one who hangs on the board glass to yell out instructions to their kids and gets thrown out of the rink. Some associations have even banned all spectator parents from the arena when their children's game is being played to avoid extreme parental behaviour. This can and does happen in all sports, in all countries everywhere. I can already hear the Americans reading this book citing baseball, basketball and football horror stories about heli-parents.

THE THEORY OF EXTRA EVERYTHING

ONE OF THE MOST COMMON WAYS TO KEEP UP WITH AND STAY AHEAD OF THE JONES'S in today's pursuit of excellence in the youth sport world is through specialization. The idea that if you do more of the same, more than others, you will get better faster. The idea is that if you only play one sport, you reach the pot of gold quicker than others.

To be clear, I am not an advocate of specialization, at least not specialization at an early age. To me, specialization should be discouraged any earlier than fifteen years of age, and under twelve years it should be seriously avoided. Getting multiple sport experiences offer way too many advantages for a child—for their body and mind—to discount. The only exceptions are sports where they peak at an early age (girl's gymnastics for example).

Academies in many sports, including hockey have opened in the high school systems throughout the country. These schools can be very good. They offer a more holistic approach to the athlete. Programs include high rep, low intensity skill movements, weight training, information about nutrition, and sport psychology sessions. They teach kids how to combine their academic goals with their sport passion. In theory, these academies work in collaboration with the athlete's club or high school team to avoid overtraining to minimize injuries. But the push by the helicopter parent to do more at an earlier age, prior to kids reaching their teenage years, creates problems. Best that specialization programs like these are kept for those entering grade nine and older. By then, the student (not the parent) can choose to specialize in one sport.

Where academies are not the answer, subsets of the various offerings can be found throughout the sport specific specialization groups and companies. For example, if a child has reached fifteen or sixteen years old and are in the realm of reaching their physical height, complementing their hockey training with weight training may be appropriate—if they want to do it, not if the parent wants them to. But if they haven't reached the level of physical maturity required to handle weight training, then it may be better to wait.

Weight training for athletes who are still growing into their bodies works best if the training leans towards pre-hab and functional movement vs. full on weight training. Pre-hab training means they are performing weight-training movements that prepare their bodies for repetitive actions in the sport, minimizing potential injuries. Functional movement focuses on agility—technique vs. weight. For example, working with a broomstick for several weeks to perfect technique rather than using a weighted bar and full-on free weights right away is the only way to go.

If you are considering weight training for your child, ask lots of questions. The goal of extra training should foster the love for being active. If the child isn't enjoying training, then why are they doing it?

WHAT WOULD WAYNE SAY?

What does Wayne Gretzky think about specialization? Gretzky did not play summer hockey, he played baseball and lacrosse in the summer. According to Gretzky's biography he was a very skilled baseball and lacrosse player and spring was one of his favourite times of the year!

> *If a sport has a high point of the year, it must be the first week of spring. When I was growing up, I used to love this time of year. It was when I put my hockey equipment away and I was absolutely ecstatic to see the end of the hockey season. One of the worst things to happen to the game, in my opinion, has been year-round hockey and, in particular, summer hockey. All it does for kids, as far as I can tell, is keep them out of sports they should be doing in the warmer weather. I could hardly wait to get my lacrosse stick out and start throwing the ball against the walls and working on our moves as we played the lacrosse equivalent to road hockey. All the good hockey players seemed to play lacrosse in those days and every one of them learned something from the game to carry over to the other—things athletes can only learn by mixing up the games they play when they are young.*
>
> *— Wayne Gretzky, National Post, March 2000*

SLIM ODDS

In the next chapter, I will discuss the odds of making it in the NHL and other major league sports. You often hear from just about anyone anywhere that the odds of making it in the NHL are slim. Yet, the pursuit of the dream continues. I would like to relate a story about someone who did make it. His name is Karl.

> Karl played with my son for a few years on an elite all-star team during the spring and summer months. Karl was a quiet and

> unassuming young boy. He was a bit larger than most and wasn't the best skater, nor did he have the best shot. He was one of those stay-at-home defensemen who just did his job. If you asked any parent (or player) on the team to name the ten best players, his name would rarely come up. He wasn't a flashy player.
>
> But Karl worked hard and continued to play. As the flashy players came and went, Karl stuck with it and got better. He ended up making a local Junior B team as a fifteen-year-old, then a successful four-year stint in the Western Hockey League. When he became eligible, he was drafted by the Washington Capitals fifth overall and is now one of the key defensemen for the Caps. I have not spoken to Karl Alzner since his playing days with our son, but I would imagine he made it because of his own hard work, determination and passion for the game.

This story shows us that it is almost impossible to predict who will make pro hockey a career and who won't, but it is up to the kid, not the parents.

Hockey parents can't help but compare their child to everyone else's. If they are not as good as the flashy players, they either make their child work harder, put them in extra programs, or pull them out. How can you possibly know who is going to make it at age seven, ten or even thirteen? Just because your kid scores three goals per game on average at age nine, doesn't mean they will make the NHL. You will be lucky to say they are still playing hockey at age fourteen. Recognize that the zombie-like pursuit of the NHL prize is not for the parents to pursue. It is for the kids. It is *their* choice to continue pursuing their passion through fun and the love of the game. If it takes them there, so be it. But remember what the odds are, and relax!

THERE IS LIFE AFTER HOCKEY

I WORKED WITH A GUY WHOSE SON WAS A GOALIE IN THE MINOR HOCKEY SYSTEM IN Edmonton. His son played on the same team as Jerome Iginla. Jerome is a famous twenty-two-year NHL veteran, with numerous accolades to his credit, including a Memorial Cup, World Junior, World and Olympic Gold Medals. Whenever my colleague would talk hockey, the conversation would always be about the days when his son played with Jerome.

As Canadians, we love to reminisce about the days when our sons played, and whom they played with. We love to name drop, especially those of us who have some connection with players in the NHL. The conversation often follows with the statement of why our sons no longer play. Then we think about the emotional pain we went through when we realized the dream was over.

The truth is, there is life after hockey. Kids go on to do other things, often for the better. They aren't playing hockey any more, at least not at a pro level, but they are doing okay. It is tough for those who are in the middle of the Hovering Game to see past the pro contract, but life will go on, without hockey.

To understand the helicopter behaviour of a Canadian minor hockey parent is to understand any nation's pro sport religious hovering zealots. They either don't understand the negative impact their behaviour has on their children today or in the future, or they simply don't care. If you are a self-proclaimed or closet heli-parent, consider having a conversation with a parent you know who had the same hovering behaviours you have, who had their kids in minor hockey with the same dreams. Ask them what their relationship is like with their son or daughter today. If it isn't a positive one (and I suspect it isn't), you may want to reconsider your behaviour and stick handle yourself out of the Hovering Game. If your son or daughter is in hockey or any other sport that you grew up with as your "religion," make sure they are in it for the right reasons.

FAST FIVE

1. Every country has its own version of a national sport religion like hockey.
2. Every Canadian parent dreams of their kid making it in the NHL.
3. Hockey can bring out the worst in a helicopter parent.
4. Playing multiple sports will help kids become better players in any sport they play.
5. There really is life after hockey.

"I love those hockey moms. You know what they say the difference between a hockey mom and a pit bull is? Lipstick."

—*Sarah Palin, Former Governor of Alaska*

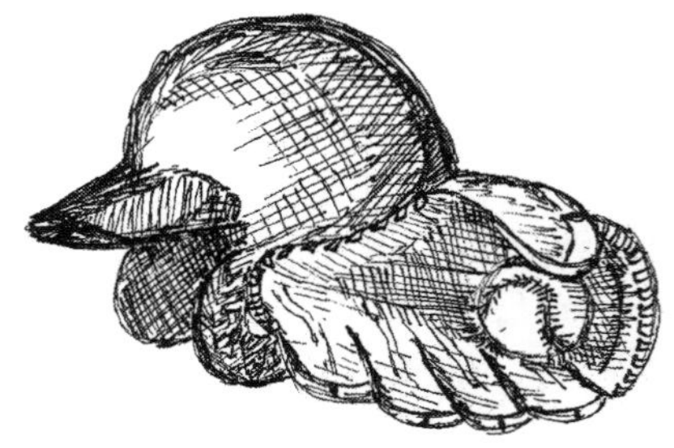

Chapter 7

Pro-Parents: Legacy Pros

"Play because it's fun, and not to become a pro. If your goal is to become a pro, the best way to realize that is by loving what you do."

—Steve Nash, former NBA Star

FOOTSTEPS

I PLAYED A LOT OF SPORTS AS A KID, BUT BY THE TIME I FINISHED HIGH SCHOOL, MY team sport of choice was volleyball. After playing senior men's club ball in Winnipeg, I was transferred with my job to Vancouver. I played volleyball in and around Vancouver almost every day, on the courts, beaches and grass. I met my wife playing volleyball. We were entrenched in the game. Our circle of friends, many are still our friends today, were all part of the volleyball scene.

When my wife was pregnant with our first, both of us still played. In fact, she competed in the University of British Columbia alumni match in late September, prior to our son being born in January. When our son was born, I remember taking him to a volleyball match between Canada and the US men's National Teams at UBC. He was only three weeks old and slept through the whole thing. When we started having more kids and raising a family, volleyball took a bit of a back seat, and we became more focused on parenting and our young children's activities.

When my oldest was in grade five, we went on a road trip to my wife's family reunion in Alberta. The event took place at our aunt's farm—hundreds of relatives, campers, tents and cars lined the long driveway from the street to the main house.

Numerous activities abounded including horseshoes, trampoline, a live band and, lo and behold, a volleyball court.

Soon after we arrived, my wife's side of the family was challenged by the other side to a volleyball match. We came from high-calibre play and knew the competition was going to be weak, so we simply played a low key game just for fun. Everyone watched the match, including our kids. When the game was over, our son ran up to us and yelled, "Wow, you guys are pro!"

Up until that point, none of our kids had ever seen us play. To us, it was just a recreational game, but to them, it was amazing. The impact it had on them that day was the beginning of their future love for volleyball. Without any prompting, they were on the road to following in our footsteps.

LEGACY ATHLETES VS. AVERAGE JOES

HAVE YOU EVER NOTICED THAT CHILDREN OFTEN END UP ON THE SAME CAREER path as their parents? Sons and daughters of lawyers, teachers, accountants, doctors and other professionals; electricians, plumbers, farmers and other labourers; police and business managers, you name it. Seems like kids tend to follow in the career footsteps of their parents. The same seems to happen in sports, music and the arts. What interests you will likely become something your children are interested in as well.

Watching pro sports of all kinds over the years, I have noticed that many of my former sport idols also had children playing in the same pro sport they competed in. Below are a few notable former major pro sport athletes and their children:

Basketball – Dell & Steph Curry, Joe & Kobe Bryant, Bill & Luke Walton

Hockey – Gordie & Mark Howe, Bobby & Brett Hull, Peter & Paul Stastny

Football – Archie, Peyton & Eli Manning, Bob & Brian Griese, Walter & Jarrett Payton

Baseball – Ken & Ken Griffey Jr, Bobby & Barry Bonds, Cal & Cal Ripken Jr.

Further research on legacy pros revealed that there are over fifty current pro team sport athletes (in each sport) whose parents played baseball, hockey, basketball and football, the four major pro sports in North America. Yet the odds of the average person making it in pro sports are astronomically low.

HERE IS A BREAKDOWN OF THE FOUR NORTH AMERICAN MAJOR LEAGUE SPORTS AND THE LIMITED ODDS OF THE AVERAGE JOE MAKING IT IN THEIR PROFESSIONAL SPORT:[9]

MLB – A high school senior who moves on to play NCAA baseball, and has aspirations to play in the Major Leagues has a 1 in 10 chance of making a pro team. Each of the thirty teams in the MLB has 25 per roster, a total of 750 players in the league. Players play an average of 5.6 years during their career.

NBA – A high school senior who plays NCAA basketball, has less than 1 in 100 chance of making it to the NBA. Each of the thirty teams has a roster of only fourteen, a mere 420 players in the league. NBA players play an average of 4.8 years in their career.

NFL – A high school senior who makes an NCAA football team, has a 1 in 160 chance of making it in pro football. Each of the thirty-two teams in the NFL has a roster of fifty-three, a total of 1700 players in the league. These players play an average of only 3.5 years.

NHL – The path for hockey is quite different.[10] While some young players have the opportunity to be selected from an NCAA school, most come from the Major Junior leagues in Canada. When you include the vast number of European internationals who are also eligible, the possibility of making it in the NHL is a mere 1 in 625. Each of the thirty NHL teams carries a roster of twenty-three players, 690 in total. The average NHL career lasts 5.5 years.

THESE NUMBERS ARE SKEWED EVEN LOWER WHEN YOU CONSIDER THE FOLLOWING:

- 70% of kids drop out of organized sport at thirteen
- Approximately 4% of high school athletes go on to play in college

So yes, the odds are very slim, but how do the legacy kids compare to these statistics?

---

[9] **NCAA.** "Estimated Probabilty of Competing in Professional Athletics", 2016

[10] **Emily Cornelius**, *"How Hard is it to Make it in the NHL?"*, 2014

As mentioned, there are over fifty players currently in each of the four North American major league sports whose fathers were former pro players. Their odds are significantly better than the average person's, all with similar odds of success.

What does the breakdown look like? What is the percentage of legacy athletes compared to the total number of current players in each of the four major pro sports in North America?

Here are the numbers:[11]

NBA – 420 pro players, 50 are legacy kids, 11.9%

MLB – 750 pro players, 50 are legacy kids, 6.7%

NHL – 690 pro players, 50 are legacy kids, 7.25%

NFL – 1700 pro players, 50 legacy kids, 3.0%

According to these numbers, three to twelve in every one hundred athletes playing now in their respective pro sports have parents who were former pros. When you compare these numbers to the Average Joes who played organized sport till they were thirteen, their odds are significantly better, probably 100s of times better! Consider that in the NBA, there are the least number of players and legacy athletes are more dominant in basketball than in the other three.

Still not a believer? Here is one of the more compelling myths out there, illustrating the unrealistic helicopter parenting plans for pro stardom.

LITTLE LEAGUE WORLD SERIES

Every year sixteen teams converge on Williamsport, PA for the Little League World Series of Baseball. Eight teams from the US and eight teams from other representative parts of the world compete in the ten-day August classic. The tournament features kids aged nine to twelve on teams that have competed in their own region (US) or country for the right to attend the tournament.

You would think that the best players in the world are at the LLWS and therefore certainly a high percentage of the players would end up making it in the Major

[11] **Wikipedia.** 2016.

Leagues in North America. Not so. Not so by a long shot. Since 1947, when the Little League World Series started, almost forty athletes have ever made it to the Big Leagues.[12] That's about half an athlete per year.

Yet, thousands and thousands of parents continue to have unrealistic goals for their kids at such an early age. Really, how can anyone know if a twelve-year-old is going to make in the MLB? If you have had, or are having these delusions of grandeur for your child in any sport, maybe the goals should be your kids' goals exclusively, not yours. Consider how you are supporting their dreams.

THE LEGACY ADVANTAGE

So how do the children of professional athletes make it? I wondered if there was any correlation between a professional sport athlete becoming a parent and their kids making it as a pro as well. What do they do differently from the rest of us? Do they have an instant advantage because their father was a pro? Is there nepotism in professional sports? Is it because they coach their kids? Are they extreme heli-parents? I wanted to find out more.

I interviewed one-on-one a group of former pros who are now parents. Some now coach in their former pro sport league, some coach their kids, and some don't. Regardless of their background or the sport they came from, their responses had an uncanny similarity.

Based on the interviews, I have determined that these former pros do provide their children greater odds of making it in their former sport or any other pro sport for that matter.

HERE ARE THE MOST COMMON FINDINGS OF THE FEEDBACK:

Focus on Effort – Teachers who are parents want their kids to get good grades in school, but as long they work hard and get an A for effort, that's what they are most proud of. They know that if the effort is there, the reward of good grades will come. It is the same for pro athlete parents. They don't care how many baskets their kid sinks, how many goals they score, or how many

[12] **Littleleague**, "From Little League to the Majors", 2016.

touchdowns they get. They are more focused on them working hard. They know that if their child puts in the effort the rewards will come.

Less Pressure – Ex pro parents emphasize more fun and love for the game. Do they push their children to compete? Yes, they do, but not in a way that impedes their passion to play. Do they give advice? Yes, but not the kind you think. They do give technical advice when asked by their child, but only if asked, and they don't force it. They do "play" with their kids, which brings out the passion naturally. They do give advice on how to work hard. What they don't do is put pressure on them. They simply try to let them enjoy the game, why? Because that's what they remember doing as kids. No pressure, just having fun.

Sharing Best Practices – All like-professionals hang out together. Lawyers hang out with other lawyers, teachers with other teachers. Pro athletes do the same. When they socialize, they talk about "like" problems, including family issues. When conversation turns to children and youth sports, they talk about things like, what sports they have their kid in. Are the kids playing other sports or just the parents' professional sport? Are they coaching their kid? Are they having fun? How do they "coach" them? As teammates, they share best practices on how to raise their kids in the youth sports world, from their perspective. Because they have all lived or are currently living the life of a professional athlete, they are able to provide advice to their child that no average kid could obtain. Long after they retire from professional sports, their network of teammates stays intact, the advice they have given to their kids holds true and if they desire it, the odds are good that they will join the pro ranks as well.

Being Around the Game – Living day-to-day with a father who is in pro sports gives the child a unique insight on what it takes to make it. All ex pros understand from being behind the scenes, what it takes to get there and to stay there. Their kids are surrounded by the pro sport culture every day, seeing how to walk the walk and talk the talk. What seems foreign to those outside the pro culture, is to an ex pro's child, just normal behaviour. It's almost like getting free on-the-job training.

Buy-in – Imagine your son being bombarded by coaches, scouts, friends and their parents, all telling them what to do to make it to the pros. It can be overwhelming and intimidating. But when your dad can say that he's been there, it is easier for the child to buy in to whatever they are preaching. The ex pros said that it seems their children buy into the love of the game because they see, hear and feel it from their parents. However, pro parents know that if their kid doesn't show passion for the game, it's hard to make it.

Sport is the Safe Haven – The life of a professional athlete has its pros and cons. One of the cons is the fact that they could move at any time. Player trades result in uprooting families and moves to new cities. It is part of their way of life. It is always hard on the family, especially when kids are involved. Pro athletes learn that during the upheaval of a trade and the move to a new city, the key thing to do for the kids is to get them registered and involved in sport activities. Sports are the common force for pro athlete children. It's where they feel safe. It's where they meet new friends and where they can continue to do what they love without worrying about other things. As a result, their kids become more adaptable to change and gain perspective. They worry less about the negative social side of things in sport and just focus on the joy of the game and the competition.

About Good Genes – Okay, this is more obvious than earth-shattering, but it is true. Most pro athletes possess the genes that give them a better chance than most of us. However, many other athletes whose parents were not pros make it as well. It just helps in increasing the odds of their kids making it. But I wouldn't get too hung up on this one. If all of the other points are not followed, the gene pool isn't going to help.

Whatever legacy you as a parent provide for your child, be it a college athlete, a professional coach, an Olympian, all of the above are constants. The odds are better for your child than for others. It's how you approach it that will make the difference for your kids and yourself.

NOTE: **Helicopter Ex Pro Parents:** *These are rare exceptions, but they do exist. These parents have either been swayed by Hovering Game players or have let their inner helicopter persona take over their parental behaviour. They get caught up with the ridiculousness of the pursuit of excellence and forget about where they came from. Best advice for them is, talk to your alumni, they will set you straight!*

FAST FIVE

- Whatever your profession is, the odds of your children following in your footsteps are better than the average.
- Legacy pros love the game their parents played.
- Did you have fun today?
- Did you work hard?
- Pro kids learn how to compete without pressure.

"The attempt to prevent our kids from struggling for fear it might scar their permanent records is, instead, scarring them for life."

—Heather Choate Davis, American Writer

Chapter 8

The Pursuit of Varsity College Sports

"You are the only one who can make a difference. Whatever your dream is, go for it."

—Magic Johnson, NBA Hall of Famer

FROM CHILD BIRTH TO COLLEGE

DREAMING ABOUT THEIR CHILD'S FUTURE IS A NATURAL INSTINCT FOR PARENTS. Parents dream about: What career path they will take? Who will they marry? Where will they live? How many children will they have? Helicopter youth sport parents dream about: What pro sport will their kid play? When will they win an Olympic medal? What university team will they make? Will they receive a full ride scholarship to college? As someone who works with families guiding them through the college sport process, I have a unique perspective to share.

When the oldest child in a family starts to think about college and playing for a varsity sports team, their parent is like a mother going through pregnancy for the first time. She reads the books, researches articles on the Internet, listens to the doctors and nurses, and garners advice from her family and friends. Even with all this information, three things are certain: One, the advice is broad and varied; two, the mother can't possibly absorb all of the information coming her way; three, what actually happens during pregnancy isn't exactly what she thought it was going to be.

Finding the right school fit for son or daughter is a similar process, yet the process of selecting a school based on making a post-secondary sports team is different and probably more difficult to navigate—there is far less information available on how to make a college team than giving birth to a child. The support network doesn't exist. The parent graduated from college twenty years ago and things have changed. There are few books or articles written on the subject. There are specific rules and guidelines in the NCAA and other college associations about recruitment and playing varsity sports. However, there are still plenty of variations that exist within the thousands of schools within these educational institutions.

Once parents have gone through the post-secondary selection process, they are far more knowledgeable the second time around and do things differently (much like the second or third pregnancy; once you've done it before it can be easier). Unless of course they are heli-parents who haven't learned from their mistakes. Many parents have no idea what to do and they often get bad advice, fuelled by their own helicopter parenting behaviours and the hovering ways of others.

PINNACLE TEAMS

MOST DREAMS AND THE PURSUIT OF EXCELLENCE GET AMPLIFIED WHEN AN ATHLETE makes an all-star or travelling team. It is great fodder for the helicopter parent, who now has their dreams and beliefs justified by their son or daughter being selected. However, the success of their child making a team like this becomes an exercise in fantasy, as more often than not, it does not lead to future success in their child's sport endeavours.

> In the sport of volleyball in Canada, National Championship competition between provincial all-star teams starts at the 16U (under sixteen) age category. Many kids who play club volleyball consider this to be the pinnacle of opportunity for them at this age. In their minds (and their parents' minds) they believe that if they make the provincial team, it is a ticket to post-secondary volleyball and a scholarship.
>
> My youngest daughter grew up with her brother and sister playing volleyball at an elite level. Her brother made all the provincial teams right through to college and beyond, so she had set her sights high. Her goal, her only goal was to make the provincial team. At the tryouts, a three-day affair, there were eighty girls who stayed in college dorms together—she made lots of friends in a short period

> of time. She loved the experience and desperately wanted to make the team. She had a good tryout, but she was not selected.
>
> As parents, we were there to watch, for support (and transportation). We did our best not to hover, and while we did have opinions, we kept them to ourselves. We did not, nor would we ever consider any kind of interference with the selection committee or coaches. It's not our way, and our daughter would have to make it on her own merits.
>
> Not being selected for the team (along with several other athletes who she thought should have made it) was devastating. The three-hour ride home was long and quiet. It was like all of her dreams were shattered. "I'll never play post-secondary volleyball now," she thought.
>
> When we arrived home, she started messaging with one of her friends who also didn't make the cut. The conversation was about them not playing volleyball anymore. As a parent, I couldn't help but "creep" behind her on Facebook. I needed to step in. I told my daughter and her friend via Facebook messaging that making the provincial team is not a prerequisite for playing post-secondary volleyball. You have to come back and work even harder to reach your goals and dreams. It is all part of the journey.
>
> Both girls ended up continuing to play. That summer my daughter's friend (and her partner) won the provincial championships for beach volleyball and went on to compete at the national beach championships in August. They soon forgot about not making the team. Both my daughter and her friend went on to play post-secondary volleyball, both on teams that won a National Championship in their respective college leagues.

There were many girls at the provincial team tryouts who were not selected but who ended up playing varsity volleyball. Of the twenty-four athletes who were selected that season, eight did not end up playing post-secondary volleyball and another four quit after their first year. Yet annually, an average of about sixty players from British Columbia go on to play post-secondary volleyball. A lot can change between grade ten and first year university.

Every time a child is *not* selected to the pinnacle team of their sport, panic sets in for the parent, not the child. Yes, sometimes, to the kid it is the end of the world. But they get over it. They choose to work harder and try again. Why? Because if they have love and passion for the sport, they will always win out in the end. But helicopter parents can't help themselves. "The selection committee and coaches are wrong, my child is better than her child—they don't know what they are doing." By reacting this way, the parent is only teaching the wrong lessons to their kid: If things don't go your way, blame someone else. Take no responsibility for your own actions. Not a good parenting method, is it?

THE FANTASY LETTER

MANY YOUTH ATHLETES AND THEIR PARENTS SEE POST-SECONDARY SPORTS AS AN opportunity for their child to get a "free ride" for tuition and education. This idea can be considered misguided, but when colleges send out recruitment letters, it really clouds reality.

It continues to amaze me how often parents new to the game of varsity sports are misguided by an NCAA recruitment form letter. For example, if a volleyball team competes at a high profile 16U tournament, many NCAA coaches and/or their scouts attend the events. They obtain the player contact information and after the tournament send recruitment letters to the identified athletes. Parents will come up to me weeks after the event and boast about how their daughter has received eight letters from different schools. The helicopter parent behaviour kicks in and they equate the letters to "they want my daughter and they will pay with a scholarship." The reality is, these are form letters that are sent out by the coaches to hundreds of potential athletes. This is not a promise of a scholarship or making a team. But the helicopter trait takes over and the parent can't help but believe the former. When the parent and athlete follow up they discover there is a lot more involved than they thought, and few of these form letters ever lead to anything good, let alone a full scholarship.

If you get a letter, do your research. For a start, go to the school's website and see where they are located, and what their academic and varsity sports programs are like. If you are interested, follow up with the coaches, visit the schools (if they are in your area) and meet the coach and the players. If they are interested, you will know. It's like a first date or interview. You will know within the first five minutes if there is more to explore in the relationship. Then and only then should you start getting (somewhat) excited about a fantasy letter offering you the world from a college.

ABOUT SCHOLARSHIPS

I'M NOT GOING TO GO INTO THE TECHNICAL SIDE OF ACQUIRING SCHOLARSHIPS, however I will say this: Your child's focus should be on getting a good education in what interests them at a reputable school. If there are several schools offering the academic program that interests them, together with the right sports program, then you are on the right path.

For varsity sports consider the coach, the players on the team, the culture of the program. Will the program fit your child's style of play and personality? These are the most important things, not the value of the scholarship. You have a better chance of getting an academic scholarship than a sports scholarship. I tell athletes to get good grades. If they have a high grade point average, it is more likely the coach will consider the athlete. Why? Because, they have a better chance of making it through the four or five years of the academic grind than those who are not as skilled academically. If they have good grades, they are more likely to qualify for an academic scholarship and the sports scholarship could come with it. Consider the sports scholarship a bonus.

There is much misinformation out there about how easy it is to obtain a sports scholarship and what it will cover relative to tuition and all of the other costs. Most parents assume they will get a full ride, but it doesn't always work that way. But heli-parents believe their son or daughter will be "the one."

It used to be that the pursuit of playing pro or post-secondary sports began the athlete's eleventh or twelfth grades in high school. Now, with the increasing number of parents playing the Hovering Game, the pursuit starts much, much earlier. And this pursuit can lead to untold stress and anxiety for the child.

Kids should be playing sports at a young age for fun. How can anyone possibly predict that an eleven-year-old is going to be a pro? How can you say your daughter is a pitcher, when she is only eight? How can you say your taller-than-average son is going to play college basketball when they are only thirteen? Don't start forcing dreams of college on your child, at least not until he or she is in high school and demonstrates a desire to play post-secondary sports—and they are doing well in school.

WHAT ARE THEY LOOKING FOR?

WHAT DO UNIVERSITY AND COLLEGE COACHES LOOK FOR IN AN ATHLETE? TALENT? Size? Height? Strength? Being the star on all of the winning teams? I speak to so many of these coaches on a regular basis, and they are all looking for the same things.

Natural Athlete – Excels in whatever sport they try—you know the ones.

Culture Fit – Fits the team culture the coach has created.

Coachable – Listens and adapts to the directions of the coaching staff.

Competitive – Possesses a high performance mindset.

Academia – Can handle the rigours of college academics and varsity sport.

Your child's talent and ability are less important because coaches can (and will) reshape their skill set anyway. If an athlete possesses these attributes but brings with them baggage (like a hovering helicopter parent), they could very well not be considered. And the worst part about it is, you will never know.

A LETTER TO YOUR CHILD

KIDS ARE VERY IMPRESSIONABLE AT ANY AGE, EVEN IN THEIR TEENS. A CHANCE meeting of a hero in their sport, who says something to motivate them, can create a goal-setting passion in them that is unstoppable. I love when this happens. It stirs up the best in a person. Dream big. But most kids don't get lucky and meet that person. The people who have the most influence are their parents. Sometimes hearing things from someone else can make all the difference. Here is my letter to your child who wants to move on to play post-secondary sports:

Hey Kids,

So you want to play post-secondary sports. What an awesome goal! Whatever the pursuit in your sporting life is, whether we are talking about making an Olympic team, playing for your local university varsity team or playing a professional sport, you need to be realistic with your dreams. But you can still dream big. There is nothing wrong with that. Just make sure you have done your research.

Be prepared to put in more time than you ever have—time in your chosen sport and your field of study, as well as the management of time itself. As a varsity athlete, your course load will be twice as heavy as the average student because you will have less time to study and socialize, as you will be devoting much of your time to your sport. Expect to study late at night, get up early, eat on the run, meet deadlines, get good grades, and of course perform well in your sport.

Post-secondary sport is a great experience. You will be part of a team of athletes who are just like you or older. Both groups will help you in your quest for success. And besides, what could be better than playing the sport you love at a high level?

So if you get there, congratulations! Jump right in and learn from all of your new life experiences. Next year it will be that much easier with one year of school under your belt.

Cheers!

Shane Donen

FAST FIVE: MYTHS AND FACTS

MYTH: "My son is going to make the NHL, and I'm going help him every step of the way."

FACT: Highly unlikely, and you're NOT helping. The sooner you treat the dream as theirs, not yours, with a bit of a reality, the BETTER chance your kid has of making it.

MYTH: "My kid is a quarterback, that is the position he plays, and he will always be a quarterback."

FACT: Kids constantly change positions. It is NOT your decision; it's between their coach and them. That holds true from five to twenty-five years old, any league and sport.

FAST FIVE: MYTHS AND FACTS CONT'D

MYTH: "College coaches are looking for players with great talent."

FACT: What they are looking for are coachable, competitive individuals who will do well in school, fit into the team culture, have good character and are natural athletes.

MYTH: "If I attend my daughter's interview with the coach to make the team, she will make it."

FACT: If you attend the interview with her, you are a helicopter parent, and she won't. Give your daughter the opportunity to take an independent stance and meet with the coach on her own. If you absolutely must attend (or if you are invited by the coach to attend) be more of a listener. Treat it as an information interview, not an interrogation or a rally to get your daughter elected.

MYTH: "My son will never make it to play varsity soccer at a college, he's not good enough."

FACT: There are plenty of opportunities to play varsity sports for athletes. If they have the passion and work hard, the opportunities will create themselves. It is just a question of where they want to play. Even if they don't make it, but they end up going to a post-secondary institution, they will get an education and set themselves up for success in the future.

"Life is more than just a volleyball game."

—Priscilla Guberman, Mother of Four

Chapter 9

Ode to the Parent Coach

"A coach is someone who tells you what you don't want to hear, who has you see what you don't want to see, so that you can be who you have always known you could be."

—Tom Landry, former Dallas Cowboys, Head Coach

THE BEST LAID PLANS

LENA WAS A FORMER UNIVERSITY ATHLETE WHO PLAYED FOUR YEARS AT LOUISIANA State University with their varsity basketball team. Many years later when she became a mother, and her daughter entered grade eight, the school's athletic director found out Lena played in college and asked her to coach. She accepted and looked forward to mentoring the young girls on the team.

Most, if not all who are in the know about basketball would say Lena's daughter was one of the better players on the team. Lena did not want anyone to think she was favouring her daughter, so she went out of her way to play her equally (sometimes less than equal) compared to the other players. They finished their season second in their league.

The school required Lena to select a Most Valuable Player for their team. Lena didn't want to show any favouritism to her daughter, but she wanted to be fair. She suggested to the team that they choose the MVP by voting in a closed ballot; the girls collectively agreed. The results of the vote would be announced at the athletic banquet at the end of the year. It turned out that Lena's daughter won by a clear majority, hence the award would be given to her daughter.

Lena's daughter received the award at the banquet, on stage with the rest of her teammates. Walking back to their team table, Lena overheard one of the players say, "Well we sure know why *she* got the MVP." Another player responded with, "But we all voted on it, didn't we?" The player said, "Sure we did, but you know how things go."

I have a soft spot for parent coaches. I was one, though I tried to avoid coaching my kids whenever possible. But not everyone volunteers, nor do they meet the minimum qualifications so sometimes you end up coaching by default.

Parent coaches are extremely common these days, especially in the early adoption team sports. CNBC published an article that cites a stat available from the Minnesota Amateur Sports Commission; approximately 85% of coaches who are dads are coaching their own kid's team in community-based programs.[13] This is due to the ever-challenging problem of not enough coaches to go around.

Associations throughout Canada and the US do their best to educate and certify coaches to give them the proper training to coach. The programs are getting better, but it is a difficult task to keep up with parental expectations—especially heli-parents' pursuit of excellence, in the Hovering Game. I will say it now, these coaches are doing the best they can, and a pretty damn good job overall at that.

PARENT COACH: COACHING STYLES

I LIKE TO DESCRIBE THE DIFFERENCES IN THE PARENT-COACH'S COACHING STYLES using three definitions:

THE FAVOURING-MY-OWN-CHILD COACH: This coach, often unintentionally, yet sometimes deliberately favours his own child. He is the one whose kid gets to play forward in soccer (all the time) and shoot the penalty shot. He is the one whose child takes the technical foul shot, the only one who seems to get to play centre in hockey, and quarterback in football, and the one who always seems to be on the court, field or ice when the game is on the line. The extreme favouring coach is the one who wants to be the head coach to make sure her son or daughter get ahead of everyone else.

CONSEQUENCES: There may be good reasons for the coach's actions,

[13] **Mark Koba**, *"Spending Big on Kids' Sports? You're Not Alone."*, 2014

but they should know that they are under every parent's microscope, especially the leader of the heli-parents. The coach's child is already at a disadvantage, being the coach's kid, so why make it more difficult for them socially. It is bad enough that the parents gossip, but their talk will ultimately end up finding its way through to the rest of the kids on the team. This coach may argue that their kid is the "best" on the team, but it is a team sport. Best for them to rethink their approach.

The Tougher-On-My-Child Coach: This coach goes out of her way to be harder on her own child than any other. This is the coach that makes her own kid do an extra set of lines, the one who seems to be scrutinized, blamed and spoken too more aggressively by the coach than any other kid. Sometimes this coach will be harder on them to avoid the scrutiny of the heli-parents. She treats her kid differently—expectations are higher, because their mom or dad is the coach.

Consequences: Being tougher on their own children isn't going to make them play better. If they see that they are treated the same as the rest of the kids, they will perform, often better than the rest because they tend to listen to the coach more than the average kid on the team—because their mom or dad is the coach. Passing judgement on how the coach's child is being treated compared to the rest of the team is a constant behaviour of other team members' parents. When parents see this excessively tough behaviour, they know it isn't cool and it becomes a distraction. Helicopter parents eat this up for breakfast. They love to stir the pot. Give them a coach who is too hard on their own child, and they will talk and talk about the coach-child relationship behind the coach's back, keeping away any potential negative focus (harm) from their own child.

The Fair-Play Coach: This coach treats his child the same as the other kids on the team. If you didn't know who the coach's child was, you wouldn't be able to pick him out (other than resemblance) when watching the team play. They are part of an "equal play-time" philosophy—each kid on the team play the same amount of time. In fact, this coach rarely puts their kid on the court or field when the game is on the line (even if they are one of the better players), partly to appease the parents (mostly the heli-parents) who are "timekeeping."

Consequences: To me, this is the best approach for the coach and their child, and for the majority of parents on the team. The coach gains the parent group's respect and thus can focus on coaching fairly. However, consequences still prevail with one or two hover parents who make their lives difficult by questioning their actions. When things don't go well (from a win-lose perspective), these parents immediately blame the coach for not playing their own child enough or the coach's child too much. These heli-parents will hover low enough to stir up the ground of the average parent and try to make something out of nothing, causing unnecessary stress for fair-play coach.

AND THE SURVEY SAYS

PARENTS ARE A TOUGH AUDIENCE. IT'S NOTHING LIKE WHEN THEY GO TO A CONCERT, say and decide whether they like the music or not. In their kid's youth sport, they have a stake in the performance because it is *their* child performing. When the performance doesn't go well, they immediately want to lay blame on someone, somehow or somewhere. Inevitably, in it becomes a "coaching issue."

In the past, our volleyball club has run an annual post-season survey in which the kids and parents respond to a series of questions about the season and the coaches. The survey was used to help improve the coaching and the club's system. One coach received the following four post-season (separate) comments from parents:

- "The team spent too much time working on skill development, and not enough on team play."
- "There was too much emphasis on team play at practice and not enough skill development."
- "The coach played everyone evenly, so we were not as competitive as we could have been."
- "The coach often did not give everyone a chance to play, some players played more than others."

This team finished second in the province in division one and ninth at nationals. Not an easy feat in any sport. At what point is it not the coach's fault? Only if they win everything? What about all the teams who didn't win? Is their coach bad? The parents were welcomed to come to any practice, and often they did, but usually showed up for the last twenty minutes or less. How can they judge what is being done at practice by only seeing the end? And when did these parents become the expert sideline or spectator coaches? I wonder what *their* practice plan would look like? How would they coach their kid, with all of the other pressures that come with coaching, and for that matter, life in general? And why should there be pressure anyways? Because their fourteen-year-old son or daughter is going to make it to the pro ranks? Seriously?

Now, consider all of the above, and plug in a new variation to the story. Imagine this is now a parent coach. Imagine the additional pressures that would be put upon them. Helicopter parents always seem to find a way of diminishing the successes of any coach by keeping the focus on their own child. This type of behaviour is damaging to so many parties at so many levels.

When parents watch a game or practice, they are effectively taking snapshots of what is happening with their kid. They can't see all that is going on—it just isn't possible for a parent to do this (hard enough for the coach to do), And even if the parent has the experience or knowledge to see the big picture, they choose not to take a panoramic view, they are focused on their own child. These snapshots are used by the helicopter parents to justify criticism of the coach when things aren't going the way they think they should for their child.

ABOUT PARENT CODES OF CONDUCT

ALL YOUTH SPORT ORGANIZATIONS HAVE SOME SORT OF CODE OF CONDUCT FOR the athlete, coaches and parents. Parent codes are distributed by email, on websites, on paper, and at parent meetings. I find that while they are written extremely well and with good intentions, they often fall on deaf ears. Parents will sign the document, but not read it, read it with an attitude of "that doesn't apply to me" or don't attend the meetings when the parent code is discussed.

Parents please read and adhere to these parent codes. They were put together with a lot of thought. If you expect the coaches to adhere to their codes, you need to do the same.

HOW TO WORK WITH THE PARENT COACH

I AM A SOLUTION-BASED PERSON. WHEN SOMEONE COMES TO ME WITH A PROBLEM that in their mind is not solvable, I always say to them, "be a part of the solution not a part of the problem." So how do you do this? How can you help the parent coaches be better and have a better experience?

HERE ARE A FEW WAYS YOU CAN BETTER HELP YOUR CHILD'S COACH:

Be Thankful – Tell your kid's coach that they are doing a good job, frequently. Say it with conviction, because they are! Recognize that your child's coach is not only a volunteer; he or she is also a parent responsible for your child and all the others on the team, including their own kid. They may have taken the job because no one else would. You may have been told this at the beginning of the season, but you may have forgotten. Remember to appreciate them for all of their volunteering. Whenever you have an opportunity, just say thanks!

Be Supportive – Coaches can always use an extra hand with something. Help with food, emails, driving, cuts and bruises, whatever it is. If you hang out at volleyball practice all the time, do something, like shag balls for the coach (but let the coach, coach).

Be Understanding – All coaches make mistakes. They are human, just like you!

Be Realistic – Your child is the "best" player, or one of the best on the team (how can he or she not be, they are your kid!). But remember, all the other team parents feel exactly the same way about their kid. A coach has to try to meet the needs of all of the "best" players on the team. If your child has an issue, be it play time, position, or a conflict, get *them* to speak to the coach, instead of you! Don't get them to text or email the coach, they should meet with the coach directly. Not in the middle of the game, wait for the right time—before, after or on long breaks during the game. If the coach can address the problem at the time, they will. Otherwise they will rearrange a time to speak with them. Giving kids a chance to solve their problems instead of interceding will teach them a lot.

Be a Parent – Parents should coach attitude. That is part of your responsibility as a parent. Don't expect your child's coach to take on parenting duties—skill coaching is their responsibility (not yours).

ADVICE FOR THE PARENT COACH

If you are a parent coach, or thinking of becoming one, read the quote from Dr. Alan Goldberg, Sports Performance Consultant. Alan works with athletes and teams in all sports from professional to Olympic level. Dr. Goldberg specializes in helping athletes and parents develop a healthy and successful sports relationship.

> *The best advice I would have for any parent who ends up having to coach their own child is to sit down before all the practices or games start and talk openly about the situation. Talk about all the pitfalls and the confusion with roles. Let your child know that it will be difficult and that you will need to work together to make it work. Ask your child what he or she would need to make the relationship work better. Part of this "better working" involves trying to keep the parent and coach role as separate and clean as possible. This means that you say to your child, "when I am on the field or court with you I have my 'coach hat' on and when we're done with the practice or game I now have my 'parent hat' on." What this may mean for you as a parent is that outside of practice you can't be pushing your child to practice extra, talk about her technique, or criticize the things that she may have done wrong in practice or the game. If your child wants to bring the sport up fine, but as the parent-coach, you must not do this.*
>
> *—Dr. Alan Goldberg, www.competitiveedge.com*

FAST FIVE

- Parent coaches will always be an integral part of youth sports.
- Kids' perceptions of coaches are often influenced by their parents' comments.
- How will you support the parent coach?
- All coaches, especially parent coaches are human.
- Empathy for the parent coach will help you gain perspective on how to be a parent.

"You can't base your life on other people's expectations."

—*Stevie Wonder*

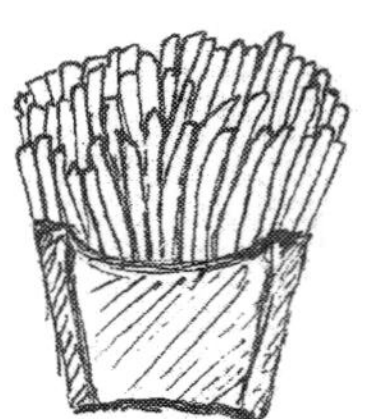

Chapter 10

Changing Behaviour

"The secret of change is to focus all of your energy, not on fighting the old, but on building the new."

—Socrates

BEHAVIOURAL CHANGE MODEL

BEFORE JUMPING FEET FIRST INTO TRYING TO CONTROL AND CHANGE YOUR helicopter parenting ways, we need to explore how and why change occurs. It is not easy to simply change your hovering habits. It takes determination and time. Let's talk about changing behaviour.

I often apply business principles I have learned over the years to coaching, parenting and managing community-based organizations. Business principles are no-nonsense, and if applied properly they can be clear and concise.

There are differences between business principles and community-based organizational principles. The most significant difference is this: In business, when you make decisions, they are ultimately between two parties—for example the relationship between the business (seller) and the consumer (buyer). But when you are dealing with community-based (sports) organizations, you are dealing with three parties, the coach (or administration of the sports organization), the children (the players on the team), and the parents of the children.

Three parties in business transactions or negotiations can occur as well. However, community-based issues are unique because you are dealing with a family unit, which adds a completely different dimension. Business principles can only hold true to community principles to a certain extent. Love and parenthood are far more complex. However, I have used one simple business model in the past that can apply, the Behaviour Change Model. This model identifies four levels of change that are essential in achieving full organizational change within a business or company. The model, illustrated below, is broken down into the four levels of change:

BEHAVIOUR CHANGE MODEL

Level 4	Organizational Behaviour
Level 3	Individual Behaviour
Level 2	Attitude
Level 1	Knowledge

To apply the model, you need to complete each level and move from one level to the next, onward to the right and upward. The levels are best explained as follows:

Level 1: Knowledge – I have acquired the knowledge to change.

Level 2: Attitude – I have taken the attitude to change.

Level 3: Individual Behaviour – I now have made the change behaviourally.

Level 4: Organizational Behaviour – Everyone in the group has made the behaviour change.

To successfully complete the Behaviour Change Model takes time and commitment. To better illustrate how the model works, let's look at a well-known example of how change became second nature in a company's organizational behaviour.

HAMBURGERS & FRENCH FRIES

When you go to McDonald's and order a hamburger, how often does the staff serving you ask if you want fries with your burger? I would say 98% of the time, which is incredible if you think about it. So how did this organizational behaviour change come into play?

In the early days, during training, new counter employees at McDonald's were provided with the *knowledge of how* to upsell French fries and *why* it is beneficial to the company. To stay employed with the company their *attitude* needed to be: "I am going to upsell French fries." They put the knowledge and attitude into play, and started executing. After a while, the attitude turned to *behaviour* and the new counter staff were *always* upselling French fries with a hamburger.

Over time, all the new and existing counter staff upsold French fries and it became an *organizational behaviour change*. This change took many years to accomplish, but became so much a part of the service culture at McDonald's that when any new counter staff were being trained, they already knew that they must upsell French fries with hamburgers. Why? Because new recruits know all the counter staff at every McDonald's do it, and if they do it, I should do it to! Upselling French fries is part of the behavioural culture at McDonald's.

This type of behavioural change takes between three and seven years to accomplish, depending on the circumstances. But once it takes hold, it can be easily maintained.

GETTING OUT OF THE HOVERING GAME

Now let's apply this model to a helicopter parent story:

> John was a former soccer player and a hard-ass helicopter parent. He was on his daughter Jamie all the time. His post-game analysis was legendary. Other parents witnessed his heated analysis immediately after a soccer game, from the pitch to the car. And of course, it continued on the ride all the way home. Anyone witnessing this tirade could see by the look on her face that Jamie was not impressed. But he was her dad and she didn't want to challenge or disappoint him.
>
> At one specific game, John's father Brian came to watch. Brian, originally from England was a former soccer player himself. He had introduced his son John to the game of soccer. He had also been a hard-ass heli-parent when John was a lad. Brian enjoyed the game, cheered on his granddaughter and had fun watching her play. But Brian noticed John's post-game antics and was disturbed.

After the match, outside on the patio at John's house, Brian started up a conversation with his son. "Son, it might be none of my business, but I can't help but notice how Jamie looks at you when you are giving her the gears about the game. It gave me an uneasy feeling inside because I remember what I was like with you and I was a jerk back then. I don't want you to make the same mistakes I did."

John thought about it and though he agreed with his father, he was left with the question, "Then what do I do?" Brian said, "Why not give her a high five, say good game and just shut up?" John said, "Okay Dad I will give it a try it." Next game, John took the plunge and gave it a shot.

When the game was over, John simply went up to Jamie and said with a smile, "Great game Jamie." Jamie looked at him puzzled, as if he was sick or something, then shrugged her shoulders and moved on.

Over the next few months, John continued the same behaviour. He avoided any post-game analysis talk. He let his daughter talk about what she wanted to talk about, soccer related or not. Eventually, Jamie's game improved and she was having more fun.

John recognized that his behaviour needed to change. His father gave him the *knowledge* of how to change. John made a concerted effort to change his *attitude* and *behaviour* towards the post-game analysis exchange. Eventually, it became second nature to him. Maybe other parents on the team who exemplified similar post-game analysis talk noticed his change and also realized it wasn't the best approach. What if all the parents on the team just said, "Good game." The full group or *organizational behaviour* change would be in effect.

What if, in the years to come, when a new player and their parents came to the team, all they saw was a "good game" response to the other kids by their parents, wouldn't they be influenced to some extent by them? Wouldn't some parents from the team tell them, "We don't do post-game analysis." Or it could be part of the pre-season code of conduct discussion by the coaches. What if parents of other teams they played against noticed their positive behaviour towards their kids and yearned to be more like them? This would take years, but eventually you would have a positive organizational behaviour change.

Think about some of your helicopter parenting habits. Do you fully comprehend why you shouldn't do it? Do you feel you have a full understanding of the problem? Now, what have you done to change your ways? Are you changing your attitude towards the problem? Is it now becoming second nature?

LUKE & YODA

IN THE MOVIE *STAR WARS: THE EMPIRE STRIKES BACK*, YODA IS TEACHING Luke Skywalker about faith while attempting to remove the X-Wing Fighter from the swamp.[14]

Luke: We'll never get it out now.

Yoda: So certain are you. Always with you what cannot be done. Do you hear nothing that I say?

Luke: Master, moving stones around is one thing. This is totally different.

Yoda: No. No different. Only different in your mind. You must unlearn what you have learned.

Luke: All right, I'll give it a try.

Yoda: No, try not. Do or do not, there is no try.

Changing behaviour at an individual level is tough, even tougher at a team level, and most difficult at the community level. It takes a lot of effort from a lot of people. But like any change in life it is not a sprint, it is a marathon. The key is to unlearn the bad behaviour and keep trying until the good behaviour prevails and the "try" becomes "do."

[14] Yoda teaching Skywalker (Faith), 2009

FAST FIVE

- Think of a story in your life that ended up with a significant behavioural change in a group organization.
- Accept the knowledge, be determined, make it habitual, influence others.
- Commitment to change, that's the difference maker.
- Changing behaviour at an organizational level takes years.
- Luke did it! And if Ronald McDonald can do it, so can you!

"The pessimist complains about the wind.
The optimist expects it to change.
The realist adjusts the sails."

—William A. Ward, American Author

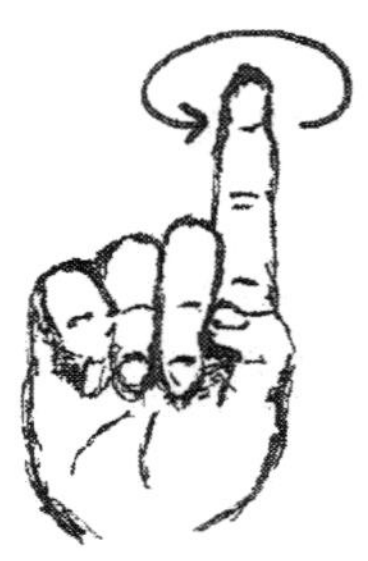

Chapter 11

How to Control Your Helicopter Behaviour

As parents, we have a very difficult job. We need to keep one eye on our children now—their stressors, strengths, emotions—and one eye on the adults we are trying to raise. Getting them from here to there involves some suffering, for our kids as well as for us. In practical terms, this means letting children struggle, allowing them to be disappointed, and when failure occurs, helping them to work through it. It means letting your children do tasks that they are physically and mentally capable of doing. Making your three-year-old's bed isn't hovering. Making your thirteen-year-old's bed is. Remembering to look for opportunities to take one step back from solving our child's problems will help us build the reliant, self-confident kids we need.

—Deborah Gilboa, M.D., AskDoctorG.com

WHICH HELICOPTER PARENT ARE YOU?

To be clear, I am not a psychologist, nor do I pretend to be. These are my opinions based on my experiences in life, the experiences of others, knowledge gathered from focus groups and one-on-one discussions, what I have read and what I have seen. I want to help individuals who are helicopter parents and those who are affected by them.

What stage of helicopter parenting are you at? Do you or anyone you know fit into one of these stages?

1. Are you the **Newbie Parent** – is this your first foray into starting your child in a sport? Is your child at an early age, entering sports for the first time? Is your child a late bloomer and has just now shown an interest in getting involved in organized sport? Are you completely oblivious to helicopter parenting?
2. Are you the **Curious, Inquisitive Parent** – your children are currently in organized sport and you are looking for a temperature gauge to see where you are in the Hovering Game?
3. Are you the **Quintessential Helicopter Parent** – had your "Aha" moments and haven't realized it yet, or have but can't get out of the habit?
4. Are you the **Closet Helicopter Parent** – in denial on the outside, but know you are deep in the Hovering Game on the inside?
5. Are you the **Drone Parent** – the stealth parent whose child has no idea what you are doing behind the scenes? Are you the one who is in constant hover mode? The one who negotiates more court time, or fights the battles for your child with the coach?
6. Are you the **Could-Care-Less Parent** – a self-proclaimed helicopter parent and okay with it? Are you curious to find out what you should and shouldn't do, or what impact your behaviours have and will have on your children?
7. Are you the **Caring Friend Parent** – is your spouse or a close friend a helicopter parent? Are you looking for ways to help them?
8. Are you the **Burned Bridge Parent** – have your children already left the nest? Is your relationship with them less than what you had hoped for? Are you looking to re-ignite a meaningful friendship with your adult children?

Regardless of what stage you are at, all of the dos and don'ts can apply to you. It's up to you to make the change. Let's get started!

DOs AND DON'Ts

IF YOU HAVE GAINED SOME KNOWLEDGE ABOUT THE PERILS OF BEING A HELICOPTER parent and want to change, work with this DOs and DON'Ts exercise to help you get started on the road to change.

First, I have listed the DON'Ts. These are helicopter parenting behaviours you want to avoid. At the end of each DON'T, you will find a corresponding DO phrase. You will find a paragraph on each corresponding DO in the second half of the exercise. Essentially, it boils down to "don't do that, instead, do this."

If you practice any of the DON'T behaviour, you are expressing helicopter parenting tendencies. If you practice any or all of the DOs, you are on the road to avoiding heli-parenting behaviour.

DON'Ts

1. **DON'T BE THE DREADED DRIVE HOME PARENT:** It is the most dangerous location in the helicopter parenting world. The car has no point of release. From the time the kid gets into the car to the time the car pulls up to the driveway, the child is at the mercy of the post-game analysis. It is the place where some of the worst behaviour takes place. Kids hate it. Don't be that dreaded parent. ***Instead, expand the topic of conversation beyond sport.***

2. **DON'T BE THE SPECTATOR COACH:** This is the parent who yells specific instructions and directives from the sidelines to their kid. "Cover the low post guy... take the shot... cover him, he's going long..." Your role is *not* to coach your child. Their coaches are coaching them. Most of the time your kid can't hear you anyways. On the rink with their helmet on, in the pool under water or on the field, far away from you, or on the court, where there is an abundance of player and spectator noise, they can't possibly hear you. Besides, there is way too much going on around them and in their heads. Further, they are supposed to be focused on the game and listening to their coach, not you. Those few children who *can* hear you don't like it much,

especially when your daughter is going to make a foul shot, and the gym is quiet, and you yell out "Make the shot, Julia." She is thinking to herself, "Shut up Dad." If you keep trying to coach her, whether you are knowledgeable in the sport or not, she will tune you out. And that can be a risky development in your present and future relationship with her. Don't be a spectator coach! ***Instead, find a distraction***.

3. **DON'T BE THE TEAM COMPLAINER:** You know the one. The parent who is disruptive in the stands, making negative comments about other players, the coaches and the referees. Often, they end up being the parent who stands alone away from the rest, because they have alienated themselves from the group. This kind of behaviour adversely affects the team and your kid. DON'T be the complaining parent. ***Instead, be a cheerleader.***

4. **DON'T BE THE TIMEKEEPING PARENT:** Some parents feel it is necessary to keep track of how much court time their child is getting compared to others and then confront the coach at the most inopportune time. If coaches are able, they try to play everyone evenly. Sometimes it just doesn't work out that way. Also there may be numerous reasons why your child is playing less or being subbed, or not playing a specific position as much as the others. Get over it—don't time keep. ***Instead, trust your coach to make good decisions.***

5. **DON'T INTERVENE ON YOUR CHILD'S BEHALF:** If you continually lobby to make sure Andrea gets more play time than anyone else, or plays the position you think she should play, there will be consequences. Eventually, your child will become dependent on you to do everything. Do you plan on driving her to her first date? Are you going to write her first essay for her (okay, their fourth essay, because you have already written the first three for them!)? Are you going to hold their hand and sit with them in class when they attend their first day of college? Rather than letting children make and learn from their mistakes, helicopter parents step in to defend their child regardless of the situation. Calling coaches or team administrators to speak on the child's behalf should be the last step in conflict resolution not the first,

and it is sending the wrong message to your kid. At what point do they get the opportunity to learn from their mistakes and become resilient? Don't intervene. ***Instead, encourage them to take control of their own destiny.***

6. **DON'T COMPETE WITH THE COACH:** Do you realize how confusing it is when you tell your son how to hold the ball when he is throwing a pitch and it is different from what the coach says? Your role is to parent. Let the coaches coach. ***Instead, try offering to help the coach.***

7. **DON'T COMPARE YOUR KIDS TO OTHERS:** There always seems to be one parent who likes to compare the skills, athletic ability, or attitudes of their child with other players on the team. They will tell other parents how their son is better than Tommy and should be on the field more. Soon the comparison carries over to their child, and he starts believing them. Resentment and jealousy ensues, all brought on by the hovering parent. A team is made up of different players, who contribute in different ways. Stop focusing on others, don't compare them to your kid. ***Instead, teach your child to be accountable.***

8. **DON'T ASSUME THEY LIKE THE SPORT:** Just because you like it, doesn't mean they do. Ask your kids if they like playing football. If they say yes, ask them why. You will know if they are being honest, or afraid to tell you the truth. Don't assume they like the sport they are playing. ***Instead, make sure they are having fun.***

9. **DON'T OVERDO IT:** Does your daughter really need to take private skill sessions at age eight to become a better basketball player? Do they have to do it five days a week? Their bodies have not fully matured until they are well into their teens. Get some perspective. ***Instead, provide them with balance.***

10. **DON'T OVERREACT TO YOUR KID'S MOOD:** Children can dramatize a situation so that it becomes far bigger than it actually is. Some parents will take this and jump to a conclusion far too quickly. Don't interrogate them because they have shed a tear of emotion. Let it go until the next day. Likely it will all blow over and you will have avoided some unnecessary confrontation with

your child's coach or a team parent. If there is something that requires further investigation, at least you will have a calmer view of the issue. Don't overreact to their mood. ***Instead, show your child empathy.***

11. **DON'T YOU OVERREACT EITHER:** Just like the child who falls, and seeing your panicked reaction starts to cry, the parent is just as susceptible to inaccurate assumptions based on what they've seen. Just because you see your daughter is crying on the bench, doesn't mean she is in peril. There are many things that could have happened. The helicopter parent in you will want to blame someone. Don't let the tears get the better of you. ***Instead, count to ten.***
12. **DON'T LIVE VICARIOUSLY THROUGH YOUR CHILD'S SPORTING LIFE:** It could be one of the hardest things to avoid, and even more so, to admit. Yesterday was your day, today is theirs. It's their turn now. Your dream will put pressure on them that is just not healthy. Don't live your dream through them. ***Instead, look for signs of their unhappiness or discontent.***
13. **DON'T TRY TO BE THEIR BEST FRIEND:** Parents who want to be the child's best friend at an early age may lose the friendship when they are adults. There are times when it is appropriate to develop a friend relationship, and there are times when it isn't. Understand the difference. ***Instead, be a parent, set boundaries.***
14. **DON'T SUFFOCATE THEM:** Our parents' rarely came out to watch our games, and while we would have liked them to be there, it was good not to have them around as well. We had to figure things out for ourselves, solve our own issues, learn to survive. You don't have to be at every game, practice or event. Give your kids the chance to be kids on their own. Don't suffocate them. ***Instead, support them unconditionally.***
15. **DON'T HOVER:** Stop the hovering. You know what I mean. How many times do I have to tell you! ***Instead, show your child how*** **to stop** ***you from behaving like a helicopter parent.***
16. **DON'T LIVE WITH REGRETS:** If you have already passed the stage of your children going through youth sports and they have

now left the nest, would you have done things differently? My guess is yes. Whatever regrets you may have, I would suggest you reconcile with your children, admit you were wrong and be at peace. But for those who are still in the game, or are about to enter the game, don't put yourself in this position in the first place. Avoid the regrets and do it right! ***Instead, just say something nice to your child.***

DOs

NOW THAT YOU HAVE READ ABOUT WHAT NOT TO DO, READ THE CORRESPONDING DOS:

1. **DO EXPAND THE CONVERSATION BEYOND THE SPORT:** On your way home in the car, try talking about something else other than the swim meet. Start with, "Did you have fun today?" Then try changing the subject to something else. "Did you know that Granddad's birthday is coming up? What should we do with him that day?" Sometimes they don't want to talk at all. If so, just say nothing. If they want to talk, they will. And that might include post-game analysis. Let your kid take the lead in the conversation—not you!
2. **DO FIND YOURSELF A DISTRACTION:** Some parents can get into the game a bit too much and their behaviour becomes disturbing. Some are so obsessed with barking out instructions to their kid—sometimes they will run right out on the ice! Instead try having a light conversation during a pressure-filled game with someone you know in the stands. Engage in a conversation while keeping one eye on the game. You will find it can be a bit more relaxing and the game will be over before you know it.
3. **DO BE THE CHEERLEADING PARENT:** Instead of complaining, try focusing on being a fan. Sounds simple enough? Just cheer.
4. **DO TRUST YOUR COACH TO MAKE GOOD DECISIONS:** Coaches have to consider so many things when putting their players out there. They have to be concerned with the health of their athletes, rules governing play time, emotional issues, teaching

moments, player conflicts, and more. Plus, often forgotten is that they are human and they make mistakes. Give them some slack.

5. **DO ENCOURAGE YOUR CHILD TO TAKE CONTROL OF THEIR OWN DESTINY:** If your child is having an issue, ask them, "Have you talked to your coach about it?" Instead of suggesting that you will immediately solve their problem by intervening, get them to deal with it themselves. You can guide and support them through the process, but ultimately empowering them to do it on their own will make a significant impact on the way they handle future conflict. If the issue isn't resolved, then the parent can speak to the coach. Fighting all their battles for them will never teach them how to fight their own.

6. **DO OFFER HELP:** Coaches will do best by your child when they, not you, are in control of the message from them. If you think you know what you're talking about, then offer coaching assistance. If they don't need your help with coaching, be the team driver, manager, food person, scorekeeper, anything. If they still don't need your help be a good fan, team parent supporter and cheer on your child.

7. **DO TEACH ACCOUNTABILITY:** If you teach your child to be accountable for their actions, (and not worry about the other kids) they will become better players and citizens in the end. And so will you. If your daughter tells you that Melissa was being lazy at practice, tell her she shouldn't worry about the other kid, and she should just work hard. If your son can't make a practice (because of an upcoming exam the next day), instead of you contacting the coach, have your son email, text or call him. Former pro athletes will often tell their own kids that if they want something, they need to work harder. If you teach accountability to your children, you will also become accountable for your actions and your behaviour in the team sport environment.

8. **DO MAKE SURE YOUR KID IS HAVING FUN:** Ask your son or daughter if they enjoy the sport they are playing, and why. If your child isn't enjoying the sport (even if you are), you need to give them the opportunity to make a rational decision whether to continue playing or not. But leave it up to them. Explain the consequences, but in the end let them do what they want to do.

If you have to drag them out of bed for an early morning practice, then it's time to have a conversation with them.

9. **DO PROVIDE BALANCE:** It's easy to let your kid engulf herself in just one activity, but soon it will become an obsession (and more importantly *your* obsession). It's important that she diversify her stimuli. If your child is constantly doing only one thing like playing video games, watching television or shooting hoops, it doesn't hurt to give him opportunities for a change of pace. Break things up with a small trip to the park, a movie, or a Skype with their grandparents. Whatever it is, do it together as a family. It doesn't always have to be hockey, hockey, hockey.

10. **DO SHOW YOUR CHILD EMPATHY:** Let him know you understand how hard it is to compete, to play hard, to make snap decisions, to get along. If he shares a story with you, share a similar story from your life experience and what you did to deal with it. You will be surprised when they remind you of the story you told them in years to come. Kids remember many things, good and bad. Help them remember the good.

11. **DO COUNT TO TEN:** It's pretty simple: If you feel heli-parenting behaviour about to spill out, just count to ten. It gives you an opportunity to remember why it is bad and you will stop. Do it when you are at the gym, in the car, at the dinner table, at the bar. No matter where, no matter what. Count to ten. Don't be a helicopter parent!

12. **DO LOOK FOR SIGNS**: When a kid no longer wants to get up to go to practice; when they seem disinterested, it's time to move on. Many people advise that if a child wants to quit a sport, they should finish the season first. Unless there are extenuating circumstances, I tend to agree. It's about integrity—fulfilling a commitment, being a team player, staying with the ship.

13. **DO SET BOUNDARIES:** You start to do this when your children are babies. What they can touch, where they can go, what they can do, and what they can't. Whether you use the word "no", distract them from the action, or some other method, you set boundaries. When they are in sports, be sure they know what

they can and can't do. "Yes you can shoot a few extra foul shots, no you can't go to John's house after practice, because it is a school day." Coaching teens, I find it best to treat them like adults when they want to push the envelope by acting like children and vice versa. They start to understand that it is okay to act like a kid in some circumstances but expected to act like an adult in others. The same goes for parenting. Don't let your kids' "entitlement generation" persona take over your parenting style.

14. **DO SUPPORT THEM UNCONDITIONALLY:** Whatever the results, be it win, lose or draw, whether they had a good game or not, whether they worked hard or just went through the motions, whether they were having a good time or were not happy, you must support them... you as parents have a responsibility to reinforce positive energy in their lives. Just do it.

15. **DO GIVE YOUR CHILD PERMISSION TO STOP *YOU* FROM BEHAVING LIKE A HELICOPTER PARENT:** If you can't help carrying on with hovering tendencies, give your son or daughter the authority to call you on it. It will be another "Aha" moment for you.

16. **DO SAY SOMETHING NICE:** Instead of talking to your child about specifics of the game, try saying this, and only this: "Honey, I love to watch you play!" That's all she really wants to hear. She doesn't want to be reminded for the third time about the goal she narrowly missed or the place she finished in the race. Kids like it when parents say something nice. "I love to watch you play" is a very powerful statement. So say it! Their smile will make it all worthwhile. Try a hug, kiss or high five, now that's being nice!

Now that you have read through the DOs and DON'Ts, see where you stand. Count up what you do and don't do. Like earlier exercises, score your spouse and vice versa—every DO and compatible DON'T. Most exercises give you a percentage, but I am telling you now, there is no room for error. You can't do any DON'T. You need to work towards 100% do.

TALK TO THE HAND

WHILE LEARNING THROUGH WRITTEN INSTRUCTION (DOs AND DON'Ts) IS effective, it never hurts to try something different like adding physical gestures to get the point across. Below are three hand gestures to perform to help identify and curb helicopter parenting behaviour.

HELICOPTERING

Situation – Someone is behaving like a helicopter parent.

Hand Gesture Response – Point your first finger towards the sky, making a twirling movement, like the blades of a helicopter.

Application – The child or spouse of the helicopter parent who is in the middle of a helicopter moment should use this gesture.

Example – Mom is commenting on one of her daughter's teammates on the way home from the game. The daughter looks at her, calls her name and makes the hand gesture motion of helicoptering.

Result – The parent may first try to defend their behaviour but will stop the behaviour within a short period of time because the message is coming from the affected family members.

PEAK

Behaviour – Someone is talking helicopter-parent style in a conversation or discussion.

Hand Gesture Response – Put your hands together in a prayer position, under the chin then pull the bottom of your hands apart, making a triangle, or peak.

Application – This gesture should be used by one of the helicopter parent's family members when the conversation about the child's sport has peaked—a sign that the subject needs to change.

Example – Dad can't stop talking about the football game at the dinner table. Mom wants to change the subject. She makes the peak hand gesture. Others at the table follow suit.

Result – The parent will stop the behaviour, feel a bit embarrassed, but also recognize this was a family decision. If the conversation has peaked, it's time to move on.

"AHA"

Behaviour – Someone is having a helicopter parent flash.

Hand Gesture Response – Raise your fist in the air and spread out all of your fingers like you are releasing something out of your hands.

Application – The helicopter parent uses this gesture. It is the sign of their recognition of having an "Aha" moment.

Example – Dad is getting frustrated watching his son's basketball game. He sees him dogging it up the court, and is about to yell out something derogatory. He catches himself, realizing that it would not be cool. He raises his fist in the air with the hand gesture.

Result – It's just another way for someone to see the light. The hand gesture is a symbol of recognition and release of tension.

Share these gesture ideas with your family. Make a plan to curb hovering. It works!

EMPOWERMENT

When our son was in grade six, a boy in grade seven was bullying him during recess. Partly psychological and partly physical, but it was definitely bullying. There were supervisors on the grounds, but there were so many kids, it was difficult to manage. When he told us about it, we asked him why he didn't defend himself. He said, "I don't want to get into trouble with the principal and get suspended from school."

So what should a parent do? Do we let him work it out on his own? Do we intervene by confronting the bully? Do we lay blame on the recess monitors? Do we report it to the principal? The next day I visited the principal's office. I told him that our son was being bullied during recess. I told him that we had instructed our son to do

> whatever was necessary to defend himself if the bullying continued. I wanted to make sure the principal was aware ahead of time, so he could advise the recess supervisors and know that this would not be a surprise to anyone. A pre-emptive strike, in case it got out of hand.
>
> Later that day, when our son came home from school, I told him about my conversation with the principal. I told him that he had our permission to defend himself if necessary, and the principal was well aware. We do not condone violence, nor would our son fight unless provoked. We condone and promote self-confidence. There are many ways to defend your self in these situations. We chose to let him figure it out.
>
> The next day, our son went to school with renewed confidence. He was not going to be bullied anymore. He became empowered. Turns out, the problem disappeared. He was carrying himself in a way that exuded confidence. Since then, he has never been bullied again.

Whether you agree or disagree with our method, the point of the story is sometimes kids need to be allowed to work out things on their own, to learn how to be resilient and survive in various social situations.

FAST FIVE

- Change does not happen overnight—it takes focus, hard work and concentration.
- Avoid the DON'Ts.
- Practice the DOs.
- Hand gestures can be powerful tools to remind you of your hovering tendencies.
- Involving your family in decisions to change behaviour will help immensely.

"Take control of the time you have
with your kids as one day they will be all grown up
and have their own friends and things to do.
Cherish every moment you have with them now as
you might not see them as they get older.
It becomes their schedule not yours!"

Kevin McCarty, American Politician

Chapter 12

Youth Sport is Good

"A lot of parents will do anything for their kids except let them be themselves."

Banksy, British Graffiti Artist & Activist

In the previous chapters, I talk a lot about the benefits of sport, from the professionals' points of view all the way through to what kids think. One theme predominates, *fun*. But is fun enough? For the kids' sport is just another activity, along with school, play, or family time. But youth sport can spawn those dreaded helicopter-parenting tendencies. So is it really worth getting your kids involved in sports? Is it worth all of the post parent-child relationship risk? Of course it is. The risk is worth the reward.

The following four stories will help keep it all in perspective.

THAT FIRST HOME RUN

> One of the best memories I have as a parent is watching my son hit his first home run in baseball. He couldn't have been more than nine years old. My wife was unable to be at the game, but I was there to witness it. I don't remember as much about where he hit the ball

or how far it went, as I do him coming around third to home plate. I was standing and cheering from the stands facing the first baseline. Rounding third, coming for home, his eyes were fixed on me all the way, grinning ear to ear. I went down to the fence and met him after his teammates congratulated him. The first words that came out of his mouth were, "I wish Mom could've been here to see that!"

These are pinnacle moments for kids and for parents that should be celebrated. We don't need to legislate these moments, they will happen. Whether it's through a child's own hard work, good coaching (from their coaches), encouragement, love and support (from their parents), or circumstantial luck, these moments will occur. What will you say to your kid during these moments? Just tell them how much you love to watch them play!

THE CHINESE FIRE DRILL

About eight years back, I was coaching a 17U team I took to Ottawa for the Volleyball Club Nationals. We were on our way back from the day's matches; both coaches were driving mini vans with six players in each van. Our vehicle was stopped at a red light and the other team van was directly ahead of us. One of my players was sitting in the front seat (my most "introverted"). She turns to me, excited and says, "Coach, can we do a Chinese fire drill?" I had a weak, impulsive moment and said "sure." She and a few other girls quickly jumped out, ran up to the other team van in front of us, banged on their windows, ran around, rapidly headed back and jumped in before the light turned green. This is a Chinese fire drill, for those who have never heard of it. All I could see from my vantage point was the van in front of us was shaking from side to side. Essentially they scared the crap out of their teammates (and the other coach). When they returned to the van, I never laughed so hard in my life!

If you ask any of those players about their memories of our season that year, it was all about the girls, their friendship and camaraderie. We won silver at provincials but that was an afterthought for them, and for me. It wasn't the medal—it was the special memories that will last the girls a lifetime. Memories like the Chinese fire drill.

FOR THE LOVE OF ART

My youngest daughter, like my other two children was an athlete. I guess she would have been classified as a jock. She played many sports throughout her youth, but eventually leaned towards volleyball. She played four wonderful years of university volleyball and was even part of a National Championship team.

My wife and I loved watching her play and have great memories of her experiences. I coached her in club for a couple of years, and did my best to minimize coaching her outside of the practice and team environment. But as a parent coach with volleyball knowledge, I couldn't help but analyze her play, especially at the college level, even if I did it internally. I deterred myself from giving advice when she played; I just supported her as needed. When you know a sport and your child plays it, you have an inner desire to help. The more you help, the more you hover. So why am I telling this, and how does this have anything to do with art?

One of her hobbies growing up was photography. When she was just fifteen she started taking pictures of her older brother's volleyball matches in high school and quickly acquired the knack and passion for taking action photos. When she entered university, she majored in Liberal Arts, and took a couple of electives in Art History and a painting course in her first year. She thought it might complement her knowledge and passion for photography. By the time she was halfway through her second year, she decided to major in Fine Arts.

Over the next four years, our athlete became an artist. She thrived in Fine Arts, majoring in paint and mixed media, and ended up graduating with honours. The following year she was accepted into another university's Masters of Fine Arts program with a full scholarship. I don't have a background in Fine Arts (if anything, I was a musician), and I don't know the first thing about art. But I do know our daughter is passionate about it. I love to watch her and marvel at what she creates. I have very little advice to give her because I don't know anything about it. I often find myself telling her, "Honey, I love to see you create your artwork." In turn, she asks for my advice, mainly about the business side of things (my expertise).

I think that parents are more patient with kids doing sports or any other activity when they know absolutely nothing about it. It is so much easier for us to relish in our children's joy, passion and successes when we don't have to (or have the expertise to) offer advice. Sure we can have an opinion, but we don't feel the need to play the Hovering Game, because we are not the experts.

I am completely fulfilled without having the expertise to offer my daughter with her art. I don't need to hover; I can just relax and enjoy the view.

FOR THE LOVE OF SPORTS

My middle daughter played club and high school volleyball. She had aspirations of playing university sport like her siblings, but she really had her eyes set on attending a specific college.

Unfortunately, it wasn't in the cards for her. Was she disappointed? Sure she was. But she loves the game more than that. She just loves to play. In fact, as a young adult, she plays more now than my other two. She plays for fun. She is competitive, no doubt about it. But she gets it. She is the best example I know of why I

> so strongly advocate participation in sports for young people. And she, like my other two children, coaches volleyball to pass on their passion for sport.

Youth sport *is* good—especially if it continues into adulthood. Don't stop playing the sport you love. Keep playing, because it keeps you in shape and socially connected with people. Most of all keep playing because it's FUN.

If you want a true gauge of how much helicopter parenting has impacted your children, see whether they still play the sports they played when they were younger in the future. If they do not, you may have had a significant part in that departure. If they are, congratulations, you got past the Hovering Game.

FAST FIVE

- The only risk you are taking by not allowing your children to participate in sports is the risk of lost experiences that last a lifetime.
- A child's smile is worth a thousand words.
- Youth sport is about long-lasting friendships, not the medal count.
- If your children have lost a passion for something, encourage them to find something else to be passionate about.
- If they play because they love to play, it's all worth it.

> "Just play. Have fun. Enjoy the game."
>
> *—Michael Jordan*

Chapter 13

Bringing Down the Helicopter

"Sometimes you will never know the value of a moment until it becomes a memory."

Dr. Seuss

THE 12 STEPS

NOW THAT YOU'VE READ THIS FAR, IT'S TIME TO GET TO WORK! TIME TO PUT THE knowledge into practice. Time to bring down the helicopter parenting aircraft hovering over your kids. Time to make a change! The following 12 Steps will help you organize your thoughts and apply knowledge to practice. If this doesn't pertain to you personally, then apply the process to your spouse or friend. Refer back to the noted chapters to help guide you through the steps.

STEP 1: **Ask** yourself why you watch your kids play organized sport. Remember why you played and why you think it's important now. Keep your decisions child-centric, not parent-centric *(Chapter 1).*

STEP 2: **Check** with your kid. Ask your child why they play sports? If they answer as most kids commonly do, you are on the right track *(Chapter 5).*

STEP 3: **Take** the Hover Test. Determine what helicopter behaviours you have or haven't yet demonstrated but could. Be honest with yourself, as you would want your child to be honest with you *(Chapter 3).*

STEP 4: **Understand** your fears. Why are you hovering or having helicopter-parenting thoughts *(Chapter 3)*?

STEP 5: **Recognize** the consequences of helicopter parenting. To understand what the long term effects can be will help you see clearly and know whether you are taking the right or wrong path *(Chapter 3)*.

STEP 6: **Determine** what stage of helicopter parenting you are at or where you might be heading. Remember, everyone has helicopter tendencies—you need to identify yours *(Chapter 11)*.

STEP 7: **Find** your "Aha" moments. Learn from these subtle but critical flashes of light in your life. If one doesn't come to mind, ask someone close to you *(Chapter 4)*.

STEP 8: **Learn** from the pros and their legacy kids. If they can do it, you can do it too *(Chapter 7)*!

STEP 9: **Leave** the dreams for the kids. Not for you. Avoid the temptation of living vicariously through your child's life *(Chapters 7 and 8)*.

STEP 10: **Practice** the DOs and avoid the DON'Ts. It can't be simpler than that *(Chapter 11)*.

STEP 11: **Change** your behaviour. Use the knowledge, make an attitude adjustment and start changing your behaviour today *(Chapter 10)*!

STEP 12: **Obtain** feedback from your spouse and kids on how you are doing. If the feedback is good, congratulations, if not, revisit a few steps and start again.

NEW HOPE FOR MILLENNIALS

WHAT WILL THE NEXT GENERATION OF PARENTS OF YOUTH SPORT KIDS BE LIKE? What will they have learned from their parents' mistakes? I sat down with Jeannie Campbell, a friend of mine from years back to talk to her about *The Hovering Game*. Jeannie is a former high school vice principal and counselor and holds a Masters in Counselling Psychology and is currently working as a counsellor in private practice specializing in relationships between kids and parents. After our discussion, I asked her if she wouldn't mind sharing her thoughts on paper. Here is what she said.

"It is my hope that as our children, the millennials, become parents, they will do it differently from the "hovering" parents we are seeing now. Millennials who are in professions are now witnessing the indulged, anxious child/youth who cannot survive without their parents holding their hand and making decisions for them and this is causing them to question the parenting that is happening.

For the most part the millennials had parents who helped them but who also held them responsible for their actions. They did not rescue. Their parents are part of the boomer generation and they were often brought up in strict homes. "Children must be seen and not heard".

The helicopter parents today are parents who are either late boomers...(born in the '60s) or the Gen Xers. The Gen Xers are to some degree a lost generation. Growing up they had permissive parenting, lots of freedom with little structure and witnessed the start of the breakdown of the family structure. Many of the Gen Xers were not able to break into the professional work force because of the overabundance of boomers, so they now want to make sure their kids get ahead.

Helicopter parents may also be the first set of parents who lived through family breakups; the hurt and confusion that this caused has made them feel the need to hover. Their emotional attachment and needs were not taken care of so they want to make sure the same thing doesn't happen to their kids. The problem is they are not going about it in the right way. They are doing for and constantly praising, which is giving kids the wrong message.

Millennials have had structure and responsibility growing up. They have had parents who were there for them but not in an overbearing way (both parents working). They went to daycare because there were no grandparents there to take care of them and they were taught to have a voice. They also understand the technology that is being thrust on people and are aware of the pitfalls. Their parents were parents, not friends while they were growing up. They will not have the disposable income to indulge their children especially if they live in the major centres. Their lives will be very different from their parents' lives.

> *The key to them parenting differently will be the need for their parents to take a back seat and let them do it their way, and this generation (in my opinion) will not be afraid to tell us so! We taught them that.....!!"*
>
> *—Jeannie Campbell, Family Counsellor*

She nailed it! Hearing from professionals always puts things in perspective. I agree with Jeannie. I too believe there is hope for the millennials. I have already seen it with my kids and the way they are approaching life. Bravo, Jeannie, Bravo!

IT'S ABOUT FAMILY

WHEN YOU COME RIGHT DOWN TO IT, IT'S ALL ABOUT FAMILY, THE RELATIONSHIP between you and your children. If it is really important to you (and heck, it should be), learn from your parents—what they did right and what they did wrong. Your parents will help shape your parenting skills.

My mother's goal in life for our family has always been to make sure that my brothers and sister and I all get along. Whenever I am speaking with my mother, she inevitably asks the question, "Have you spoken to your brothers or sister lately?" To be honest, I feel the same way about my adult children. I want them to get along, always. But I also want to have open, honest relationships with them. I want them to feel they can talk to me about almost anything. And I want them to know that it's okay *not* to tell me everything, just know I am there if they need me.

In researching this book, I have been fortunate to find and insert so many great quotes from so many famous people, but I have left my own quote till the end.

May *The Hovering Game* inspire you to change your helicopter parenting ways. Change yourself, change your community, change the world.

"Life is more than just a Hovering Game."

—*Shane Donen*

ACKNOWLEDGEMENTS

FIRST AND FOREMOST, I MUST ACKNOWLEDGE THE VAST CONTRIBUTORS BY ALL the people connected with youth sport for backing up my assumptions. Being a sports administrator, I have had the advantage of seeing many families before, during and after the upbringing of children, and unfortunately I have also seen the trials and tribulations of helicopter parenting. Associations work tirelessly to improve policy, procedure and process to stop the spread of parental hovering, but they are fighting a losing battle. I have had many one-on-one meetings with coaches, professional athletes, parents, principals, athletic directors and counsellors. I have conducted my fair share of focus group sessions with parents, grandparents and children. Their passion for the topic is unprecedented and current. Without their input, I never would have even considered writing this book.

You can't publish a book without an editor. Who knew? But if your editor is good, you can create something special. Marnie is a great editor. Her patience and direct approach pushed me to take the book to another level. Thank you for your guidance.

You can't truly appreciate life as a whole unless you have friends. I like to define a friend as someone who, even if we haven't seen or spoken to each other in months, or years, when we do get together we just start where we left off. A friend doesn't worry about who hasn't called whom. A friend is someone who will sometimes just listen without sharing his or her own problems. A friend is someone who comes to the aid of another without any second thoughts. I have those kinds of friends. Many of them. You are the backbone of my existence. You all know who you are. Too many to name, but I could not have written this book without you.

I had a great childhood. So many fond memories form the foundation for the book. My mother and father, my brothers and sister, my aunts, uncles and cousins were all part of the happiness that I remember and cherish. Their love shaped me as a person.

My deepest fear was that I had demonstrated some helicopter parenting behaviour myself when raising our kids. When you write, you are putting yourself out there. During the writing of the book, I needed to ask my wife and kids the question, "Was I a helicopter parent?" To my relief, they all said, "No, definitely not."

My lovely wife and my dear children have been my biggest supporters and fans through this and all of my life. For that I am eternally grateful, and thank god I passed the test!

ABOUT THE AUTHOR

SHANE DONEN IS A BUSINESS CONSULTANT, AN entrepreneur, a tireless coach and sports administrator in the Community of South Surrey, British Columbia. He is the co-founder and president of Seaside Volleyball Club, circa 2003, one of the largest boys and girls volleyball clubs in the province. He is an active member of the Regional Development Committee for Volleyball BC and a founding member of the Host Committee responsible for bringing the Women's National Volleyball Team Training Centre to Richmond, BC and the Richmond Olympic Oval. In 2009 he coached the Canadian National Women's Volleyball Team that took bronze at the Maccabiah Games, the World Jewish Olympics held every four years in Tel Aviv, Israel. He has coached club and high school at all levels, both boys and girls for over twenty years. Shane is a mentor for Canadian families of athletes who want to move on to play post-secondary varsity sports through his company, Pursuit Mentorship Services. He is a certified Level 2 volleyball coach, working on his Level 3 certification. Shane, and his wife of thirty-five years, Maryanne have three children, Kyle, Jillian and Mallory. All three children are also actively involved in coaching and playing the sport of volleyball. The four of them are his beacon of light, the ultimate joys of his life in this wonderful sport-minded family.

FOR MORE INFORMATION, CONNECT WITH SHANE ON HIS AUTHOR'S BLOG AT HELICOPTERPARENTING.NET

STORYTELLING

I am a storyteller at heart. It's what I love to do. I think it stems from my teenage years as a singer-songwriter. I used to write ballads inspired by the songs of Jim Croce and James Taylor, telling stories in my own way, hoping they would appeal to the listener. When I ventured into the real world to earn a living, I worked my way up the ranks in retail, from serving customers to managing staff, to middle management to leading organizations. Throughout all of my experiences, I was always in storytelling mode, training my team using stories to get the point across. I have used storytelling in my coaching life and personal life. It's what I am truly passionate about. If I can tell a story that results in helping people, then I have accomplished my goal.

—Shane Donen, June 2016

NOTES AND RESOURCES

4 **Active Healthy Kids Canada,** *Report Card on Physical Activity for Children and Youth,* 2014. http://www.rbc.com/community-sustainability/_assets-custom/pdf/AHKC-2014-Short-Form-Report-Card-English.pdf

Almendrala, Anna. *"5 Signs You Were Raised by Helicopter Parents"* Huffpost Healthy Living, www.huffingtonpost.com WEB. 30/9/2015.

6 **Bayless, Kate,** *What is Helicopter Parenting?* Parents.com, 2013. http://www.parents.com/parenting/better-parenting/what-is-helicopter-parenting/ WEB. 2013.

10 **Cornelius, Emily.** *"How Hard is it to Make it in the NHL?"* Huffpost Sports, 2014. http://www.huffingtonpost.com/emily-cornelius/how-hard-is-it-to-make-it_b_5803634.html WEB. 11/11/2014.

Costa, Brian. *"Why Children are Abandoning Baseball"* The Wall Street Journal. www.wsj.com. WEB. 20/5/2015.

Engagesports. *Effective Management Strategies for Youth Sports Leaders.* E-book. http://www.engagesports.com/e-book

7 **Ewing, Martha and Seefeldt, Vern,** *Institute for the Study of Youth Sports,* Michigan State University, 1990. http://activeforlife.com/top-five-reasons-kids-play-sports/ WEB. 17/4/2012.

Gilboa, Deborah, M.D. www.AskDoctorG.com

5 **Ginott, Haim G.,** *Between Parent & Teenager,* Macmillan, 1969. See also: www.between-parentandchild.com

Goldberg, Alan. *Competitive Advantage, Peak Performance and Overcoming Sports Fears and Blocks.* https://www.competitivedge.com

8 **Hodgkinson, Mark,** *"Nightmare Tennis Parents Who Don't Play Ball"* The Telegraph, 2008. http://www.telegraph.co.uk/education/3356561/Nightmare-tennis-parents-who-dont-play-ball.html WEB. 21/6/2008.

1 **Kelley, Bruce.** *"Hey, data data – swing!"* ESPN, 2013. http://espn.go.com/espn/story/_/id/9469252/hidden-demographics-youth-sports- espn-magazine WEB. 11/7/2013.

[13] **Koba, Mark.** *"Spending Big on Kids' Sports? You're Not Alone."* www.CNBC.com 2014. http://www.cnbc.com/2014/01/13/youth-sports-is-a-7-billion-industryand-growing.html WEB. 13/1/2014.

Langhorst, Paul. *"Youth Sports Participation Statistics and Trends"* Engage Sports Engagesports.com WEB. 3/8/2016.

Lee, Alice. *"7 Charts that Show the State of Youth Sports in the US and Why it Matters"* The Aspen Institute. www.aspeninstitute.org. WEB. 24/2/2015.

[12] **Littleleague.** *"From Little League to the Majors"* Littleleague.org, 2016. http://www.littleleague.org/Little_League_Big_Legacy/Little_League_World_Series/From_Little_League_reg__to_the_Majors.htm WEB. 2016.

Miller, Rob. www.proactivecoaching.com

[9] **NCAA.** *"Estimated Probabilty of Competing in Professional Athletics"* NCAA. NCAA.org, 2016. http://www.ncaa.org/about/resources/research/estimated-probability-competing-professional-athletics WEB. 25/4/2016.

O'Sullivan, John. *"The Race to Nowhere in Youth Sports"* Changing the Game Project. www.changingthegameproject.com. WEB. 24/3/2014.

Participaction, *The 2015 ParticipACTION Report Card on Physical Activity for Children and Youth* https://www.participaction.com/sites/default/files/downloads/Participaction-2015ReportCard-FullReport_4.pdf WEB. 2016.

The Physical Activity Council, *2016 Participation Report,* http://www.physicalactivitycouncil.com/PDFs/current.pdf WEB. 2016.

[2] **SFIA**. *Sports, Fitness, and Leisure Activities Topline Participation Report.* 2016. http://www.physicalactivitycouncil.com/pdfs/current.pdf

[11] These figures came from my calculations of stats found on Wikipedia in May 2016

[3] **USA Hockey,** *Membership Stats.* 2015. www.usahockey.com http://www.usahockey.com/page/show/839306-membership-statistics WEB. 2015.

Wallace, Kelly. *"How To Make Your Kid Hate Sports Without Really Trying"* CNN www.cnn.com. WEB. 21/1/2016.

[14] Yoda teaching Skywalker (Faith), Youtube, Oct 23, 2009 https://www.youtube.com/watch?v=7YkbgvRMpWO

Made in the USA
San Bernardino, CA
26 July 2016